Paul Laurence Dunbar.

PAUL LAURENCE DUNBAR

PAUL LAURENCE DUNBAR

Poet of his People

By

BENJAMIN BRAWLEY

Chapel Hill

1936

THE UNIVERSITY OF
NORTH CAROLINA
PRESS

To MADRE

WITH WHOM I FIRST READ

THE POEMS OF

PAUL LAURENCE DUNBAR

Preface

THE following pages attempt to give a biography and a critical estimate of the young Negro poet who became famous just as the last century drew to a close. While Dunbar is in a general way familiar to all, it is surprising to note that comparatively little independent study of his life and work has been made. In his last years he was visited more than once by Mrs. Lida Keck Wiggins, and the account of the poet's life which that author wrote was included in the subscription edition of the poems and stories published in 1907. It excelled in anecdote and in acquaintance with the letters, and has served as the basis of numerous secondary sketches. I am indebted to Mrs. Wiggins and her publisher, J. L. Nichols and Company, for permission to use the letter of Dunbar to Dr. Tobey included in Chapter III.

I am especially under obligation to the poet's mother, Mrs. Matilda J. Dunbar, and his sister-in-law, Mrs. William Murphy, whose co-operation it was my privilege to have. On one never-to-be-forgotten morning in July Mrs. Dunbar gave me access to the poet's scrapbooks and others of his treasures, assuring me, as I was well aware, that it was not in her power to do more to show her sympathetic interest. Her courtesy was a benediction, now cherished more than ever, as she has since joined "the choir invisible." Mrs. Alice Dunbar Nelson was also very kind, taking any time or pains necessary to help me to be accurate; and Mr. Richard B. Harrison informed me about Dunbar's early efforts in the field of the drama. One recalls with regret that these two valiant spirits also can now no longer speak to us as they once did. Professor and Mrs. Kelly Miller, Mr. Edward F. Arnold, and Dr. Amanda V. Gray Hilyer, all of whom were friends of the poet in Washington, have assisted on special points; and Mrs. Dorothy B. Porter, keeper of the Moorland Collection in the Howard University Library, and Miss Caroline L. Jones, of the Collis P. Huntington Library at Hampton Institute, have endeavored to place at my disposal all available material. I am also indebted to Professor R. W. Tibbs, of Howard University, and to Mr. H. T. Burleigh, who have assisted me in connection with the pieces which have been set to music, and to the authors who have permitted their poems to be included in the section "The

Praise of Dunbar" in the Appendix.   To all who have
so graciously helped I extend my thanks.   As is indi-
cated in the course of the work, the quotations from
Dunbar's poems are used with the permission of and
by special arrangement with Dodd, Mead and Com-
pany, Inc., the authorized publishers.

Benjamin Brawley.

WASHINGTON, D. C.,
   February 9, 1936.

CONTENTS

PAUL LAURENCE DUNBAR

When all is done, say not my day is o'er,
And that thro' night I seek a dimmer shore:
Say rather that my morn has just begun,—
I greet the dawn and not a setting sun,
When all is done.

I

The Poet and His Age

THIS is the story of a young Negro who struggled against the most grinding poverty, who never completed his education as he desired, and who yet became famous when only twenty-four years of age. For two or three years his success was so great that it became a vogue. Born in Dayton, in the Middle West, he had only limited opportunity to study the Negro; yet he gave a better interpretation than any writer who had preceded him. Moreover, by his fine taste and his ready wit he won the approval of the most cultured and discerning. The whole phenomenon of his career is one of the most notable in the history of his people and the nation.

If one will go to Dayton, walk half a block north from the station, and take a car going west on Fifth Street, after riding for about a mile and crossing the

Miami, he will come to Summit Street. If at that
point he leaves the car, diagonally across to the left he
will see the new Paul Laurence Dunbar High School,
a beautiful and impressive building of light brick first
occupied in the autumn of 1933. Going to the north
and passing from South to North Summit, after four
blocks he will come to Number 219. This was the
last home of Dunbar. The house is a modest one of
brick, two stories in height and shaded by a large
maple. The porch on the left, on both sides of which
are fretted iron supports, opens into the living-room.
From the spacious yard, also on the left, one can see a
grape arbor in the rear. There is nothing pretentious
about the place: if it were not for the tablet in front
it might not be noticed; but already for more than a
quarter of a century it has been a shrine.

All because the man who lived here gave to the
world a song. When he died, Brand Whitlock tele-
graphed to his mother: "You have lost a son; I have
lost a friend; but America has lost more than all else,
and that is a poet."

It is the poet who fathoms for us the mystery of
life. Sooner or later every man asks the meaning of
the daily struggle, the reason for his infinite effort.
Deep too is the hope of reward. This may be a well
deserved holiday, a home for which one has striven, or
the fruition of a great enterprise, perhaps even a new
romance. Often, however, we do not win the prize,
and hope and wait indefinitely. Meanwhile we may

have our joy vicariously. When then there appears one who can speak for us, we hail him, for we know he too has yearned and striven. If he has not reached the stars, he has at least had the vision. We may have to bear with him; he is not always bound by convention and may even defy our routine: but we will forgive, for he too has often hoped and loved in vain.

Such a man is God's best gift to a nation. He doubles men's joys and halves their sorrows. When they are baffled and uncertain, he bids them gird themselves anew and go forth to a high destiny. He is no mere maker of verses. He is, as Carlyle said, a prophet as well as a poet. Communing with beauty, he also walks with truth. There is no mistaking him, for the mark of heaven is on his brow.

It was this that Paul Dunbar meant to his people and to some extent to his country about the turn of the century. One morning he received a letter from a woman in a distant city. Her father, she said, had been killed in a railway accident and for years after the event her mother had not smiled. Then one day somebody in the house read aloud "When Malindy Sings"; and the mother, swept on by the humor and the melody, suddenly broke into laughter. After that she faced life with new courage, and the whole family felt indebted to the man who had wrought the change.

He thought like a poet and worked like a poet.

The slightest suggestion—a sound, a picture, a gesture—was sufficient to call a poem into being.   One night in Colorado there came to him through the dark the sound of a herd of cattle slowly plodding their way onward.   Suddenly he thought of a race struggling to the light.   He began, "Slow moves the pageant of a climbing race"; and thus was born "Slow Through the Dark."   To a little maiden he knew in Massachusetts it seemed that the "woo-oo" of the east wind was the call of "the Boogah Man," and this was enough to make him build for her a poem on the theme.   "The Eastern Shore" of Virginia was the scene of a happy vacation; and the next winter, when he was miles away and when the snow was falling, he recalled the summer days by the sands of Chesapeake Bay.

Paul Dunbar was thus a genius working in his own right.   It is also necessary, however, to consider him in relation to his age.   He appeared at a time of extraordinary import for his country and the world.   On all the great continents politics had come to the end of an era and stood on the threshold of a new day. In every phase of life mighty movements were astir, and one could not avoid a sense of impending change. No one could tell what the future would bring.

It was this contradictory temper of the last years of the century that accounted for the strange union of realism and romanticism so often found in the work of representative writers.   Science and invention were changing modes of living, and there was much that was stern or harsh if one cared to see it; but somehow the heart of the man would not be overcome. Liberal spirits were determined to live keenly and joyously; meanwhile the multitude idealized the past. Such was the mood of the hour, and it was this that sought refuge from all that was unpleasant.

The time was thus primarily one of feeling, and feeling, it proved, on the plane of common emotion. On the stage the fine art of Edwin Booth was succeeded by that of Richard Mansfield; but the actors whom the thousands flocked to see were James A. Herne in *Shore Acres* and Denman Thompson in *The Old Homestead*. The bicycle was in its first flush of popularity, and *Ships that Pass in the Night* sold edition after edition. In Chicago in 1893 was opened the World's Columbian Exposition, just forty years before the Century of Progress; and in January of that year *Trilby* appeared in *Harper's Magazine*.

It was natural accordingly that in 1890 James Whitcomb Riley should be the most popular poet in the United States. The taste of the day was for sentiment—sentiment simple, strong, and even tearful; and "An Old Sweetheart of Mine," "Little Orphant Annie," and "The Old Man and Jim" were sung or recited thousands of times. Close to Riley in spirit were Will Carleton, with "Over the Hill to the Poor-House," Eugene Field, with "Little Boy Blue," and Frank L. Stanton, with "Mighty Lak a Rose." Richard Hovey and Bliss Carman wrote *Songs from Vaga-bondia,* and Ella Wheeler Wilcox thrilled many a young and sometimes an older person with her moral-izing and her tumultuous rhythms. Meanwhile Rich-ard Watson Gilder and Walter Hines Page were prominent as editors, and William Dean Howells was distinguished both as critic and novelist.

With all of the sentiment and optimism, there was before the American people one question which, like Banquo's ghost, would not down—that of the position of the Negro in the body politic. In the aftermath of the Civil War the black man had won not only freedom but the right to vote, and within a few years Negroes sat in both houses of Congress. After a quarter of a century, however, a change had taken place. The issues before the country were no longer primarily political but social and economic, and the current that now set in was strongly against the Negro. Disfranchisement abounded, and peonage and the convict lease system flourished. When some Negroes, dissatisfied with conditions, began a move-ment to the cities, there was a tendency to make leg-islation as to vagrancy especially harsh, so that a man could not stop work without technically committing a crime. In the year 1892 alone there were 255 known cases of lynching, mainly of Negroes. All told, the period was one of the darkest in the history of the race in this country.

When, however, the Negro people were most discouraged, when they were almost demoralized by wrong and injustice, even then it was that they were given hope by some of their number who wrought well. Douglass died in 1895, but in that same year Booker T. Washington delivered in Atlanta the speech that made him famous. Flora Batson and Sissieretta Jones showed the power of the Negro voice; a capable scholar, W. E. Burghardt DuBois, appeared on the scene; and from Paris came word of a young American painter, Henry O. Tanner, who was winning laurels by his art. At the Peace Jubilee in Chicago, at a great meeting attended by President McKinley, Booker T. Washington spoke eloquently of the Negro as one who in every crisis of the nation had chosen the better part. Meanwhile John Mercer Langston in Washington and James C. Napier in Nashville represented the public spirit and the social culture to which the race aspired.

All of this seething, surging life Paul Dunbar saw, and part of it he was. When he began to work, the literary possibilities of the life of his people had been only dimly perceived by Negro writers, though among his contemporaries there was one man, Charles Waddell Chesnutt, who was a genuine rival. There was of course a reason for the fact that the Negro himself had not done more. Above any question of the black man as artist was that of his position in American life. When he felt so strongly the burden of proof, he deemed it necessary first of all to satisfy the white man's standards, and naturally he looked to the white man's models. The comedy of the life about him, especially that which called for dialect, seemed not sufficiently dignified for literary treatment. The tragedy he felt keenly, but he was not sure that he could win for it a hearing. The result was that frequently there was an artificial tone to what was written. Only rarely did one come to grips with reality.

If Negro writers had such hesitancy, however, white authors had none, and they soon realized that in the life of the people about them was a vast fund of unexploited material. Unfortunately these writers almost always started off with outworn premises. Prominent among these were that the system of society in the South before the war was admirable, that the wisdom of emancipation was debatable, and that any attempt to educate the Negro was likely to prove a waste of money. In general it was taken for granted that all effort to break away from the old life was bad for the black man. In 1876 a young author from Mississippi, Irwin Russell, had some of his dialect poems accepted by *Scribner's Monthly*. In one an old Negro lamented the evil days that had befallen his master since the war; in another a similar character gave warning to his son who was leaving home to work on a boat. Again and again the old man was the object of a joke. Russell himself soon passed from the scene, but the tradition that he represented was carried forward by the stories of Thomas Nelson Page, who dedicated to him one of his first books and who resolutely set his face toward the past. The Uncle Remus stories of Joel Chandler Harris are now a part of the folk-lore of the world, and in his later years their author took a liberal attitude toward the Negro, but in general there was nothing in his early work that was counter to the prevailing temper. Meanwhile one heard on every hand the songs of Stephen Collins Foster, "The Old Folks at Home," "My Old Kentucky Home," and "Old Black Joe"; and black-face minstrelsy was at the height of its popularity.

When then Dunbar began his work there was not only general emphasis on the sentimental in American literature, but also special emphasis on what were supposed to be the good times in the South before the war. It was natural for him to be affected by what seemed to make strong appeal, and so he was; but he soon realized the shortcomings of his models and struck a more distinctive note. He was deeper than Russell, for he understood not only the humor but also the striving of the Negro; and he was better than Page, for he had not that author's malevolence. He could not possibly have appeared at a more opportune moment. A decade earlier the public would hardly have been ready for his message; a little later, when there was more demand for realism, he might not have awakened such sympathetic response.

By the Negro people he was given a place never accorded to any other man. There have been many men of whom they have been proud, but never another that they loved like this one. He was their own. They rejoiced in his triumphs; they forgave his mistakes. They heard with breathless interest about his travels or his health. Old men in him renewed their youth; children in the lowlands thrilled to him; and young people in the schools saw in him what was possible for them. His hopes and fears, his sorrows and joys were theirs. All of the difficulties that lay before them, they saw that he surmounted. In his success all their dreams came true.

II

Early Years

Among the slaves who escaped from Kentucky to Canada by "underground railroad" in the years just before the Civil War was one Joshua Dunbar. In the light of freedom the newcomer learned to read and he supported himself by working at the plasterer's trade. Meanwhile he watched with the keenest interest the important events affecting the Negro in the United States. Returning to the country in the course of the war, he enlisted in the Fifty-fifth Massachusetts, commanded by Colonel Norwood Penrose Hallowell. This was the second regiment of Negroes recruited in the North, the first being the famous Fifty-fourth Massachusetts, led by Colonel Robert Gould Shaw. After the war Dunbar settled in Dayton, Ohio, and there, already advanced in years, he married in 1871 a young widow, Mrs. Matilda Murphy.

Mrs. Dunbar proved to be a woman of remarkable personality. She had unusual initiative, was witty, and, though without formal education, had a keen sense of literary and spiritual values. She had been born near Shelbyville, Ky., in or about the year 1844. Until the signing of the Emancipation Proclamation she was the slave of David Glass, a large planter living at Shelbyville. The home in which she worked was one of culture, and, in spite of her untoward condition, she added to her humor and her gift for description the taste for that which is best. While still a slave she was married to R. Weeks Murphy, and of this union were born two sons, William T. and Robert S. When about twenty-two years of age, having lost her husband, she removed to Dayton with her two little boys, and it was there, while she was earning her living by laundry work, that she met Joshua Dunbar. From her second marriage there were two children, one a son, the subject of this story, born June 27, 1872, and the other a daughter, Elizabeth, who died when only two years old.*

* Mrs. Dunbar outlived her famous son by several years, being about ninety when she passed February 24, 1934. Though she was feeble and her sight dim, her mind was active and bright almost to the end. Her son William had preceded his mother in death by a little more than a year. Robert S. Murphy, the father of a large family, survived her.

Joshua and Matilda Dunbar were still living on Howard Street in Dayton when their son was born. There was considerable discussion as to the name to be given the new member of the family. The father suggested "Paul"; but the mother demurred, thinking this too old-fashioned. Then said Joshua Dunbar, who had a quaint and formal way of addressing his wife, "Matilda Madam, don't you know that the Bible says Paul was a great man? This child will be great some day and do you honor." Thus the matter was settled, a middle name, "Laurence," being given in compliment to a friend of the family in Dayton.

With unusual solicitude Matilda Dunbar strove to enable the boy to fulfil his father's prophecy. She herself had learned to read and write, picking up a letter or a word here or there, sometimes from school-children; and for a while she attended a night school. When Paul was not more than four years of age, she began to teach him his letters. In later years she was asked more than once how old he was when he began to write verses. To that she could not give a definite answer. He was always scribbling, she said, and she could not tell when he was composing a poem or writing a regular school exercise. He himself said that he made his first attempt at rhyming when he was only six, and that his "first poetical achievement" was the reciting of some original verses at a Sunday School Easter celebration when he was thirteen years old. In school he showed an inclination toward literary studies, excelling in reading, spelling, grammar, and later in literature. Some influence came from pictures in the home, especially two large ones which had been left to Mrs. Dunbar by a lodger. One of these represented "The Finding of the Saviour in the Temple," and the other was a reproduction of "Hippocrates Refusing the Presents of Artaxerxes," from the painting by A. L. Girodet. To these must be added a smaller picture of Abraham Lincoln, of whom Mrs. Dunbar always spoke with reverence. Sometimes the thoughtful boy heard his father speak of the days of the war, of his own regiment or of the attack of the Fifty-fourth on Fort Wagner. Again he listened eagerly to stories of old Kentucky, unconsciously impressed by his mother's inimitable phrasing.

Joshua Dunbar died when his son was twelve years old, and the two Murphy brothers went away to work in Chicago. Even as a lad Paul was thus left alone with his mother in the home; and then and always between the two there was the deepest affection, also the most sympathetic understanding. The boy was not robust in health, rather delicate in fact, and he engaged little in outdoor sports. Even if he had been so inclined, he would have had little time, for it was necessary for him to help in the home. His mother supported herself by washing clothes or doing any other work she could get to do; and he would carry out the bundles or baskets, or help about the hotels in the city whenever opportunity offered. For some years as they worked thus, their home was on Ziegler Street in Dayton.

Even while he was in the intermediate school, there were teachers who perceived the ability of Paul Dunbar and who were interested in his progress. One of these was Samuel C. Wilson, a writer and a man of culture, to whom the young student more than once returned for advice and encouragement. In due course Paul passed to the Central High School. At the time this was the only high school in the city. Later, with a change of location, it was superseded by the Steele High School, so that it was commonly spoken of as "the old high school." At Central, Paul was liked by his classmates, who soon perceived his merit. In his second year he was admitted to the Philomathean Society, a literary organization; and he soon began to contribute to *The High School Times*. His tact and talent were such that in his last year he was chosen both president of the society and editor of the paper. Again he had sympathetic teachers. One of these, William Watkins, was among those who encouraged his poetic gift. In his regular studies he was most attracted to the poets of highly æsthetic quality, especially those whose verse was rhythmical —Shelley and Keats, Tennyson and Poe and Longfellow; but he also read with enthusiasm the popular poets of the day, chiefly Riley and Field. Of the magazines that he saw he prized most the *Century*,

to which he dreamed of contributing some day.   Thus
the years passed.   He was the only Negro in his class,
and, as graduation approached, it was clear that his
place among his fellow students was one of esteem
and even affection.   For the exercises held at the
Grand Opera House on Tuesday evening, June 16,
1891, he wrote the song, a poem of eight stanzas.

Why stirs with sad alarm, the heart,
For all who meet must some day part?
So, let no useless cavil be;
True wisdom bows to God's decree.

Though lingers on the lid the tear,
'Tis one of sorrow, not of fear,
For well we know we can not cling
Forever to the parent wing.

*   *   *   *

The wind is fair, the sails are spread,
Let hearts be firm, "God Speed" is said;
Before us lies the untried way,
And we're impatient at the stay.

At last we move; how thrills the heart,
So long impatient for the start!
Now up o'er hill and down through dell,
The echoes bring our song—farewell.

III

Aspiration

THE five years immediately succeeding his gradua-
tion from high school were the most critical in the
life of Paul Laurence Dunbar. As long as there were
lessons to get, and the completion of the course to be
kept in mind, the way was clear; but now that all was
over, what was next? He was nineteen, ceasing to
be a boy and drawing toward manhood. How best
could he develop his talent? How best could he give
of himself to the world?

Primarily, he felt, by something of a literary nature.
College by all means should be considered—perhaps
a profession, the law, or, as he later thought, the min-
istry. For the moment, however, there was the
pressing problem of earning a living and helping his
mother. Anything else must wait.

Then it was that there came to Paul Dunbar the

problem faced by thousands of young Americans since, and in his case rendered doubly difficult. [Was there anything that he could do, in an office, on a newspaper—anything of a clerical nature? No. There was no one who wanted a Negro youth in such capacity. Sometimes the answer was kind, more often it was brusque; but the meaning was ever the same.

[At last he found a place as elevator boy in the Callahan Building on Main Street. The wage was only four dollars a week, but—that was four dollars. It did not seem quite right; there were young men who had never been to high school who could run an elevator. The days were passing, however, and hunger was insistent.

One thing at least he could do, and that was to keep his vision before him. Thus it was that on August 12, 1891, there was a "dramatic and humorous recital" given by "Paul Laurence Dunbar, Dramatic Reader," assisted by local talent. The chief performer on this occasion made three appearances, and the selections he used were indicative of his literary preferences at the time. First he recited "Annabel Lee" and a scene from *The Lady of Lyons*. On his second appearance he gave Tennyson's "Lady Clara Vere de Vere," and on the third the Quarrel of Brutus and Cassius from *Julius Cæsar*. There is no indication that the recital was an unusual success.

The weeks lengthened into months, and before one could realize it, winter had come again. Meanwhile, when the day's work was over, or even as he went up and down on the elevator, Paul Dunbar would write his little verses and sketches. When sent forth, the poems were often returned. Sometimes, however, they did not come back until they were in print, first in papers in the Middle West, but more and more in journals nearer the East. "Christmas is A-Comin'" was in the Rochester *Herald*, December 24, 1891. Ever was there in the background for the young author the inspiration of his mother, all the more strong because not always articulate; and even then he had the yearning to do something that might give his people a higher place than that which they held in the nation's life.

In the early summer of 1892, it happened that the Western Association of Writers met in Dayton; and one of Dunbar's former teachers, Mrs. Truesdale, saw to it that he was invited to deliver the address of welcome. On this occasion, as more than once later, he hoped to give a routine part on the program such a literary turn as would lift it above the commonplace; and thus he resolved to speak the welcome in verse. When the hour for his number drew near, he got leave from the elevator, went to the assembly hall, and in due course was presented by Dr. John Clark Ridpath. This was his first appearance before such an intelligent and critical audience, and no one who was present that day could ever forget the simple dignity with which he walked down the aisle and mounted the platform, or the ease with which he spoke. The lines which he delivered on this occasion he dated June 27, 1892. That was his birthday. He was only twenty, and one does not have to wonder that those who heard him were surprised by his fine feeling and the aptness of what he had to say. The advance beyond the class song of just twelve months before was hardly less than amazing.

"Westward the course of empire takes its way,"—
So Berkeley said, and so to-day
The men who know the world still say.
The glowing West, with bounteous hand,
Bestows her gifts throughout the land,
And smiles to see at her command
Art, science, and the industries,—
New fruits of new Hesperides.
So proud are you who claim the West
As home land; doubly are you blest
To live where liberty and health
Go hand in hand with brains and wealth.
So here's a welcome to you all,
Whate'er the work your hands let fall,—
To you who trace on history's page
The footprints of each passing age;

To you who tune the laureled lyre
To songs of love or deeds of fire;
To you before whose well-wrought tale
The cheek doth flush or brow grow pale;
To you who bow the ready knee
And worship cold philosophy,—
A welcome warm as Western wine,
And free as Western hearts, be thine.
Do what the greatest joy insures,—
The city has no will but yours.

That was all, and he was gone. The members of the Association, however, had been greatly impressed, and they later took the young poet into their organization. The next day Dr. Ridpath and two of his associates, Dr. James Newton Matthews and Mr. Will Pfrimmer, seeking out Dunbar at his place of work, found him in the elevator, by his side a copy of the *Century Magazine,* a lexicon, a tablet, and a pencil. As he himself later described the meeting, his embarrassment was terrible; in the middle of a sentence a bell would ring and he would have to leave his guests and go up for a passenger. Before the call was over, however, Dr. Matthews questioned the poet about his life. He later secured a number of the poems and wrote for the press a letter quoting these. A copy of this letter attracted the attention of James Whitcomb Riley; and under date November 27, 1892, this famous author wrote from Denver to Dunbar as follows:

See how your name is traveling, my chirping friend. And it's a good, sound name too, that seems to imply the brave fine spirit of a singer who should command wide and serious attention. Certainly your gift as evidenced by this "Drowsy Day" poem alone, is a superior one, and therefore its fortunate possessor should bear with it a becoming sense of gratitude and meekness, always feeling that for any resultant good, God's is the glory, the singer but His very humble instrument. Already you have many friends and can have thousands more by being simply honest, unaffected, and just to yourself and the high source of your endowment. Very earnestly I wish you every good thing.

Dunbar greatly prized this letter, and he addressed some lines to Riley, hailing him as the singer of songs that came close to the heart. These he included in his first collection and they were reprinted in the *Complete Poems*. There were also lines "To Pfrimmer," written after reading *Driftwood*, and these are to be found in the same two places. To Dr. Matthews the young poet felt especially indebted—how much so may be seen from the following sonnet:

> All round about, the clouds encompassed me;
>   On every side I looked, my weary sight
>   Was met by terrors of Plutonian night;
> And chilling surges of a cruel sea

That beat against my stronghold ceaselessly,
  Roared rude derision at my hapless plight;
  And hope, which I had thought to hold so tight,
Slipped from my weak'ning grasp and floated free.
But when I thought to flee the unequal strife,
  As wearied out I could not bear it more,
  Fate gave the choicest gem of all her store,—
And noble Matthews came into my life.
  He warmed my being like a virile flame,
  And with his coming, light and courage came.

This sonnet was included in Dunbar's first collection but not in any other. He later wrote poems that were better by far, but hardly one that reveals more of his own thought and feeling, or of his effort to throw off the despair that sought to engulf him in the years of his young manhood. On the death of Whittier in September, 1892, he was moved to write a tribute; and he praised the author of *Snowbound* as one who had no need of maudlin sentiment and whose life and songs alike were "sublime in their simplicity"; but he did make reference to the poems against slavery.

As another winter drew near he thought more and more of bringing some of his pieces together in the form of a book. As different ones had appeared in newspapers from time to time, he had given these to his mother, asking her to keep them for him. When the papers accumulated, having been reproved by the neighbors for keeping them piled on a table, she put them in a box under the old-fashioned safe in the kitchen.   One evening, after a hard day on the elevator, the young author came home and asked for them; and that night he spent in selecting and arranging such poems as he wanted to use.   The next morning he announced to his mother that he intended to publish a book.   Going, however, to the United Brethren Publishing House, he was doomed to disappointment.   Already some supposed friends who had said they would do what they could for him, had either forgotten their promise or found excuse for not keeping it.   The representative of the firm to which he now presented his poems informed him that they could not be published on a regular royalty basis, that the house could not assume any responsibility, and that the collection could be printed only at the author's risk, the cost being one hundred and twenty-five dollars.   Would the firm then print the book and permit him to pay after a few weeks?   No, not unless there was ample security.

The young author had turned away and was leaving in discouragement when the business manager of the firm, Mr. William Lawrence Blacher, who knew his worth and had observed his dejection, called him to his desk.   "What's the matter, Paul?" he asked. "Oh," said Dunbar, "I wanted to have a volume of poems printed, but the house can't trust me and I can never get one hundred and twenty-five dollars to pay for it in advance." Mr. Blacher talked with him a little further and then thrilled him by saying that he would give his personal guarantee for the book and that it would be out in time for the Christmas holidays.

The young people at the high school heard of the proposed publication, and, although a year and a half had passed since Dunbar was graduated, there were those who remembered him pleasantly and who were eager to help in any way they could. On the stationery of *The High School Times,* under date October 28, 1892, several students pledged themselves to buy a copy of the book when it appeared. About the same time also the paper formally called attention to the forthcoming work:

> Mr. Dunbar has been granted the unsolicited praise of some of the greatest writers of our land. His poems have appeared in some of the widest circulating magazines and publications of the West. He will publish a volume of his poems in a short time, and every High School student should procure a copy of the works of one who, two short years ago, was among us. Subscribe your name to the struggling poet's list at the Callahan Building, or leave your name with the editor.

One snowy morning a few weeks later, a delivery man came to the home of the poet with a large package addressed to "Mr. Paul Dunbar."

"These are a few of Mr. Dunbar's books," he said. "And, by the way, what is this Dunbar? Is he a doctor, a lawyer, a preacher, or what?"

"Who? Paul?" replied the proud mother. "Why, Paul is just an elevator boy, and—a poet."

Day after day in the busy season now at hand the young man on the elevator, with a new hope in his eyes, asked those who came in if they would buy his book. More than one had reason to know him pleasantly and showed kindly interest. When some others paused and remarked that the book was a very small one to cost a dollar, the author replied with a touch of humor but also with something of confidence that it was not selling on its size but its merits. Within just two weeks after the appearance of the work he came again to the office of the Publishing House and this time placed in the hands of Mr. Blacher the full amount of his obligation, one hundred and twenty-five dollars. That was not all. In the Dunbar home it was a Christmas long to be remembered. The little book paid for, there was still money for a dinner such as the family had not had in years, and even something with which to buy a present for a friend. As Mrs. Dunbar said long afterward, quoting her son, they "jes had one scrumptious time."

The book thus given to the world bore the simple title, *Oak and Ivy, by Paul Dunbar.* The date was 1893, but this anticipated the new year, for, as we have seen, it was just before Christmas, 1892, that the

work appeared.   The little volume, once hesitatingly
offered by the author to any who would buy, is now
exceedingly rare.   As his first formal collection, it is
naturally of the highest importance in any study of
his development.

The book is neatly printed.   All together there are
fifty-six titles and sixty-two pages.   Not less than
twenty of the poems were included in *Lyrics of
Lowly Life*, the notable collection of 1896, and eleven
of these were also in the intermediate collection, *Majors and Minors*.   Prominent among those in all three
books were "Ode to Ethiopia," "A Drowsy Day," "A
Banjo Song," "The Ol' Tunes," "Life," and "Columbian Ode."   Since several pieces from the first volume
were included in the second volume as well as the
third, one can not help wondering why the charming
"October" was not given a place in *Majors and Minors*.   Seventeen titles rejected for both *Majors and
Minors* and *Lyrics of Lowly Life*, were nevertheless
included in *Complete Poems*.   Full lists are given in
the bibliographical section.   In only one instance does
Dunbar seem to have included in a later single volume
a poem from *Oak and Ivy* that he did not place in
either *Majors and Minors* or *Lyrics of Lowly Life*,
and that was when he used "My Sort o' Man" in *Lyrics
of the Hearthside*.   A few pieces, mainly some obviously imitative, were never used again.

The first impression that one gains from a reading
of *Oak and Ivy* is that of the influence of such au-

thors as Russell and Riley. This was the Dunbar that
had to be outgrown, as the poet himself soon realized.
One comes upon such titles as "The Old Apple Tree,"
"The Old Homestead," "An Old Memory," "Goin'
Back," "The 'Chronic Kicker'," and "My Sort o'
Man." In "Goin' Back" an old Negro who has lived
for thirty years in a Northern town, is at the railway
station about to take a train for the home of his youth.
He has seen much to admire in the North, but he
could not find there the passion and fire and the
genuine sympathy that he expected to find in human
beings—certainly not "the real ol' Southern hearti-
ness," and concludes,

> But now I'm a goin' back again
> To the blue grass medders an' fiel's o' corn
> In the dear ol' State whar I was bo'n. . . .
> Back to my ol' Kaintucky home,
> Back to the ol' Kaintucky sights,
> Back to the scene o' my youth's delights. . . .
> Don't mind an ol' man's tears, but say
> It's joy, he's goin' back to-day.

In some of the poems such as this the diction was
artificial, and there was even a mixture of the Hoosier
with the Negro dialect. Dunbar was later very criti-
cal of work in this excessively sentimental vein.
When, however, the matter was one of the pure ex-
pression of the joy of living, without obvious preach-

ment, he did not hesitate to use the theme that seemed best and this brings us to the second impression that one is likely to gain from *Oak and Ivy*. In "The Ol' Tunes" one finds that the poet has already struck the note that later made him famous. In this piece there is still some reminiscence of Riley and Whittier, but the smooth rhythm, the whimsical satire, and the sincerity of feeling are Dunbar's own. The man who wrote this poem was already very nearly full-grown.

The same may be said of some of the poems in classic English. The initial piece, "Ode to Ethiopia," shows Dunbar already concerned with the deeper problems of his people. "A Drowsy Day," as we have observed, was one of the first of the poems to interest the discerning. "October" is a pure lyric, lavish in its sensuous quality, and with figures in perfect harmony with the subject. The two stanzas entitled "Life" and beginning "A crust of bread and a corner to sleep in" immediately won the approval of all lovers of good verse and have since been much quoted. In general, while *Oak and Ivy* contained several pieces that suggested the imitation of popular authors, it also contained more than one poem that went beyond promise and reached fulfilment.

Not long after the appearance of the little book, Judge Charles W. Dustin, of the Court of Common Pleas in Dayton, having become interested in the young author, gave him a position as messenger in the Court House, also making it possible for him to study

law.   About the same time a review of *Oak and Ivy*
in the Toledo *Blade* attracted the attention of a rising
attorney of the city, Mr. Charles Thatcher, who wrote
to the poet, asking him to send him a copy of the
book and to tell him something of his life.   Dunbar
replied from Richmond, Indiana, where he was giv-
ing a reading at a church social in charge of some of
the prominent women of the city.   He said that there
was not much to tell, but spoke of his mother and his
work on the elevator, adding that he hoped to pay
for the little home he had bought through a building
and loan association but that most of what he had paid
had gone for interest.   He also said that he was soon
to go to Detroit for a reading.   Mr. Thatcher re-
plied at once, asking that he tarry in Toledo on his
way to Detroit long enough to see him.   Dunbar
called on April 15, 1893, and immediately impressed
his new friend by the dignity of his bearing and his
desire for further education.   While the two talked
Mr. Thatcher suggested that it might be possible for
several interested men to finance a college course, a
note to be redeemed in the future being given to each
one who co-operated.   Eager not to offend his visitor,
he thus put the matter on a business basis.   Dunbar
did not hesitate as to his reply.   He was very grate-
ful, he said, but hoped to be able to accomplish his
purpose alone.   While he was in Detroit he received
a telegram from Mr. Thatcher asking him to be pre-
pared to recite for the West End Club the following

Wednesday evening. This organization had but recently been formed, and it was the custom that at the weekly meeting some prominent person would appear for an address. Dunbar had the feeling that unusual significance attached to the occasion and he prepared for it very carefully. On the night appointed Dr. W. C. Chapman of Toledo, who had recently made a trip to the South, spoke on the Negro in that section. He took an unfavorable view and followed the general trend of the literature of the period by raising doubt as to the black man's capabilities. There were exceptions of course, he said, among them Paul Laurence Dunbar, but in general he thought that his position would hold. He did not know the young poet himself was present and was to speak after him, and was covered with confusion when it was announced that Dunbar would "favor the club with several original selections." The lone Negro rose with dignity, but with a heart on fire, and he said: "I will give you one number which I had not intended reciting when I came: it is entitled 'Ode to Ethiopia.'" That night he spoke with all the fervor of his being. It was as if one young man had taken upon himself the defense of all his people from the slurs and slanders to which they were daily subjected, and there was no doubt, when the evening was over, where the honors lay. Dunbar said to Mr. Thatcher that perhaps he showed too much feeling in reciting his ode, but there was no one else who had any criticism to make.

With the opening of the World's Columbian Exposition in Chicago in the spring of this year, the thought came to Dunbar as to many other struggling young men that perhaps he could find there profitable employment. He had already written an ode in honor of the event, and he realized that there was the possibility of a new audience. As the time to leave approached, however, he had misgivings, and, leaning against the mantel, he said to his mother with broken voice that he did not want to go. It meant his first extended stay away from home; Chicago was a great wicked city; and he was afraid. Then she who had watched over him from his earliest years and who had faith in his manhood as well as his genius, once more gave him courage, and he went forth to the battle.

Having arrived in Chicago, day after day he spent in the search for suitable employment, only to be baffled. At one time he was put to work on a dome; again he was in a room unduly damp. At length, however, Frederick Douglass, commissioner in charge of the exhibit from Hayti, employed him as a clerical assistant, paying him out of his own pocket five dollars a week. After a few weeks, Dunbar sent for his mother, and she came, did a little work on her own account, and was thus able to make a home for her son. On a day at the Exposition featuring the achievement of the Negro, he recited several poems, winning great applause and eliciting much favorable comment. He also formed a friendship with the reader, Richard B. Harrison, with whom he later made a brief tour in the effort to sell his book. Thus the summer passed.

The poet never forgot the friendly interest of Douglass at this time, and when that champion died in 1895, he paid tribute to him as one who was "no soft-tongued apologist," but who held to his vision without care for the lash of scorn or the sting of petty spite. After the turn of the century, when Dunbar's prominence in literature had brought him strongly face to face with the dispraise to which his people were subjected, he once more turned in thought to the valiant leader, calling for "the blast-defying power" of his form to "give comfort through the lonely dark."

In 1893, however, almost before he realized it, the autumn had come. The Exposition over, he returned with his mother to Dayton. The winter was near, there was little money on hand for food and fuel, and none at all for the clothing that was needed. Moreover, foreclosure on the humble home was threatened. Seeing no way out, Dunbar wrote to Mr. Thatcher, asking if it would now be possible for the arrangement suggested for a college course to be effected. Mr. Thatcher replied that he was as willing as ever to do his part but that the others who had been interested now unfortunately seemed unwilling to go forward. This was a hard blow. About the same time the poet was in communication with a man who was

organizing a Negro concert company and who wanted
him to go as a reader. For weeks he worked fever-
ishly, composing new pieces and committing many to
memory, only to be informed ten days before the
time for leaving that the whole plan had been can-
celled. He went again to Detroit for a reading, hop-
ing that this would net at least a few dollars, only to
learn that, as the affair was for charity, it had been
expected that he would donate his services. In des-
peration he wrote again to Mr. Thatcher, stating
frankly that he had no money and no work and that
the little home was about to be lost. Could some of
the money intended for his college course be sent to
relieve his present embarrassment? The appeal was
not in vain, and the home was saved. The relief,
however, was only temporary. The money was soon
spent, and the weeks that succeeded were the darkest
in the poet's life. "There is only one thing left to be
done," he wrote to a friend in November, 1894, "and
I am too big a coward to do that."

"There is a budding morrow in midnight," Keats
had said; and even then, when the way seemed darkest
to Dunbar, there were powers working in his behalf.
Miss Mary Reeve, a woman of unusual intelligence
and a book reviewer, was for some days the guest of
Dr. and Mrs. H. A. Tobey, of Toledo, where Dr.
Tobey was superintendent of the State Hospital for
the insane. One day the conversation happened to
touch upon race, and Dr. Tobey, a man of great heart

and democratic spirit, remarked that the only thing
he ever asked about an individual was what was in
him, without regard to creed, nationality, or race.
"I suspect then," said Miss Reeve, "that you would be
interested in a Negro boy we have down in Dayton.
I don't think much of him myself, but my sister says
he has written some wonderful things." *   Dr. Tobey
replied that he would not be interested in the youth
because he was a Negro, but simply for any ability he
might possess.   A few days later, after his guest had
returned to her home, he received from her a copy of
Oak and Ivy.   He was not especially impressed and
put the book aside.   Not long thereafter, however,
he was in Dayton on business and while there in-
quired about the young author.   Interested by what
he heard about Dunbar's faithfulness at work and his
eagerness to help his mother, he looked again at the
poems when he got home, and now found new mean-
ing to them.   He wrote to the poet, encouraging him
and enclosing money for several copies of the book
to be distributed to his friends.   It was two or three
days before Dunbar replied, but the letter that he then
sent is so important in its portrayal of character and its
bearing upon his life that it is here given entire:

* The sister to whom reference was thus made was
Mrs. Frank Conover, to whom Dunbar later dedicated
Lyrics of Sunshine and Shadow "with thanks for her
long belief."

Dayton, Ohio, July 13th, 1895.

MY DEAR DR. TOBEY:

If it is a rule that tardiness in the acknowledgment of favors argues lack of appreciation of them, you may set it down that the rule has gone wrong in this case. Your letter and its enclosure was a sunburst out of a very dark and unpromising cloud. Let me tell you the circumstances and see if you do not think that you came to me somewhat in the rôle of a "special providence."

The time for the meeting of the Western Association of Writers was at hand. I am a member and thought that certain advantages might come to me by attending. All day Saturday and all day Sunday I tried every means to secure funds to go. I tried every known place, and at last gave up and went to bed Sunday night in despair. But strangely I could not sleep, so about half-past eleven I arose and between then and 2 A.M. wrote the paper which I was booked to read at the Association. Then, with still no suggestion of any possibility of attending the meeting, I returned to bed and went to sleep about four o'clock. Three hours later came your letter with the check that took me to the desired place. I do not think that I spent the money unwisely, for besides the pleasure of intercourse with kindred spirits which should have been sufficient motive, I believe that there were several practical advantages which I derived from the trip, whence I have just returned.

I wish I could thank you for the kindness that prompted your action; I care not in whose name it was done, whether in Christ's, Mahomet's or Buddha's. The thing that concerned me, the fact that made the act a good and noble one was that it *was* done.

Yes, I am tied down and have been by menial labor, and any escape from it so far has been only a brief respite that made the return to the drudgery doubly hard. But I am glad to say that for the past two or three years I have been able to keep my mother from the hard toil by which she raised and educated me. But it has been and is a struggle.

Your informant was mistaken as to my aspirations. I did once want to be a lawyer, but that ambition has long since died out before the all-absorbing desire to be a worthy singer of the songs of God and nature. To be able to interpret my own people through song and story, and to prove to the many that after all we are more human than African. And to this end I have hoped year after year to be able to go to Washington, New York, Boston and Philadelphia, where I might see our Northern Negro at his best, before seeing his brother in the South: but it has been denied me.

I hope, if possible, to spend the coming year in college, chiefly to learn how and what to study in order to cultivate my vein. But I have my home responsibilities and unless I am able to make sufficient to meet them I shall be unable to accomplish my purpose. To do this I have for some time been giving readings from my verses to audiences mostly of my own people. But as my work has been confined to the smaller towns, generally the result has not been satisfactory.

Perhaps I have laid my case too plainly and too openly before you, but you seem to display a disposition to aid me, and I am so grateful that I can not but be confidential. Then beside, a physician does not want to take a case when there is reticence in regard to the real phases of it. And so I have been plain.

Sincerely,

PAUL L. DUNBAR.

140 Ziegler Street,
Dayton, Ohio.

The next month Dr. Tobey wrote to the young poet, inviting him to come to the hospital and read to some of the patients. A carriage was sent to the station for him, and the doctor awaited his coming with Charles Cottrill, a young man of Dunbar's own people and one of his friends in the city, whom he had persuaded to come to introduce the poet. As Dunbar alighted from the carriage Dr. Tobey, looking from the window, said half aloud, "Thank God,

he's black." Mr. Cottrill, who happened to be of
fairer complexion than his friend, was startled and
somewhat taken aback; but Dr. Tobey hastened to
explain, "Whatever genius he may have can not be
attributed to the white blood he may have in him."

The point that Dr. Tobey remarked was one later
mentioned many times in connection with Dunbar.
When he spoke there were those in the country who
were making every possible effort to discredit the
Negro by books and articles in the magazines and
daily press. Even some years later a student of race
problems brought out a book entitled *The Mulatto*,
the method of which was the very simple one of enu-
merating all persons connected with the Negro race
who had any degree of prominence and asserting of
very nearly all that they were mulattoes. It was sup-
posed to follow, of course, that any merit they pos-
sessed was due to their white blood. Dunbar became
the outstanding refutation of this fallacy.

The reading at the hospital was a success. In the
course of the autumn Dr. Tobey invited Dunbar to
come again. This time, having heard of Mr.
Thatcher's interest in the young author, he invited
him to be present also; and thus these two men joined
hands to further the poet's progress. On this occa-
sion Dunbar recited several new pieces which he had
composed and these especially interested his friends.
Talking with him at the close of the program they
learned that he had hope of bringing out another vol-

ume, and then and there together they generously
undertook to defray the expense of printing, all pro-
ceeds from the sale to belong to the author himself.

The book thus arranged for was *Majors and Minors*.
It was printed and bound by the firm of Hadley and
Hadley, of Toledo. The date was 1895, and the poet
hoped that his new collection might be out in time
for the Christmas holidays; but it did not appear until
early in the new year. Dr. Tobey was as eager as a
boy in looking forward to it, and even before the book
was bound he went to the printing-office, got some
of the loose sheets and cut the leaves himself. The
dedication, as in the first collection, was to the poet's
mother. On the title-page the author's name was
given as "Paul Lawrence Dunbar," but it never again
appeared thus, as he regularly insisted that the middle
name should be spelled with a *u* rather than a *w*.

As a piece of book-making *Majors and Minors* was
not as good as *Oak and Ivy*. The paper was thinner
and duller, and the selection and arrangement of type
not quite so admirable. Even one sympathetic reader
spoke of it as a "countrified" little volume. All that is
true. At the same time, if we consider only original
work, that is, the number of excellent pieces that had
not previously appeared in a book, *Majors and Minors*
becomes the most notable collection of poems ever
issued by a Negro in the United States. The next
volume, *Lyrics of Lowly Life*, was in better form and,
having a standard publisher, must ultimately be re-

garded as more important; but most of what was good in that book had already appeared in *Majors and Minors*.

There were many more titles than in *Oak and Ivy*, and a total of one hundred and forty-eight pages. The first eighty-six were given over to poems in classic English, a later section being entitled "Humor and Dialect." Dunbar felt that it was unfair for an author to use in one book what he had already used in another; hence he included only eleven poems from the first collection. Among these were "Ode to Ethiopia," "A Drowsy Day," "A Banjo Song," "The Ol' Tunes," and "Life." Among the new pieces were "The Poet and his Song," "Ships that Pass in the Night," "Ere Sleep Comes Down to Soothe the Weary Eyes," "Invitation to Love," "The Party," "The Spellin' Bee," "When de Co'n Pone's Hot," "The Deserted Plantation," "Accountability," "The Rivals," and "When Malindy Sings." Any one who could write these poems was already very nearly if not quite mature.

What immediately strikes one accordingly is that Dunbar has now found himself. The hard years through which he has passed have given him deeper insight, more confidence, and, one might add, greater sternness. With all of the sympathy and tenderness there is something of iron in him. He is quick to know when the smile may be legitimate and when there can be no suggestion of compromise. An artist is now working in his chosen medium; anything like imitation or artificiality he is rapidly placing behind him. He is a poet of sorrows as well as joys. And where did the young man who had never been South get this exquisite finish for his Negro dialect? Where but in the stories heard at his mother's knee even from his earliest years?

The initial piece is a poem in three parts entitled "Ione," the story of an older brother who was led to give up the lady for whom he cared, to a young brother who also fell in love with her. Some of the lines are reminiscent of Longfellow and some of Browning.

> She loved me, I could not mistake—
> But for her own and my love's sake,
> Her womanhood could rise to this.

One might ask, however, if Ione's womanhood should do any such thing; all is not quite clear about the ethics of the proceeding. Even if the older brother chose to sacrifice himself, it is an open question if he should ask the young lady who loved him to transfer her affection to some one else. There are also echoes of Tennyson and Lowell, and sometimes, as in the lines from "Preparation,"

> The little bird sits in the nest and sings

and

> But the note is a prelude to sweeter things,

one might ask if the suggestion is not a little too close. "Changing Time," "The Wind and the Sea," and "Disappointed" call up Ella Wheeler Wilcox; "A Border Ballad" is in the manner of Richard Hovey's "Stein Song"; and that the influence of Riley and Carleton has not wholly passed may be seen from "The Corn-Stalk Fiddle" and "Lonesome."

May be seen in

Mother's gone a-visitin' to spend a month or two,
An' oh, the house is lonesome ez a nest whose birds
    has flew
To other trees to build agin; the rooms seem jest so
    bare
That the echoes run like sperrits from the kitchen to
    the stair.
The shetters flap more lazy-like'n what they ust to do,
Sence mother's gone a-visitin' to spend a month er
    two.*

A bookish tendency was also to be seen in the use of the literary conceit, a noticeable characteristic of Dunbar's early verse and one which he never wholly outgrew. A conceit forms the basis of the popular little poem of four lines entitled "Dawn." In "Be-

* As is said in the Preface, this quotation and later ones from poems included in Dunbar's *Complete Poems* are used with the permission of and by special arrangement with Dodd, Mead and Company, the authorized publishers.

yond the Years," Night "drops tears," and even in such a poem as "Ode to Ethiopia" labor's "painful sweat-beads" are made "a consecrating chrism." On all such things of course we have to meet a poet halfway; he is expected to see more than an ordinary observer, and Dunbar seldom used phrases that he could not defend. A friend asked him if the line, "The blush went out in her blanching cheek," in "The Lover and the Moon," was not a little strained. "On the moon," he said, "I discover just the suggestion of a blush."

It is not such things as these, however, that give the book its merit. One turns instead to lyrics of superb rhythm and to poems in dialect of far more natural temper. "The Poet and his Song" is in every way typical of Dunbar's best work. It is the sort of poem that almost forces one to commit it to memory. The figures are felicitous, the diction inevitable, and the movement in perfect tune with the feeling.

> A song is but a little thing,
> And yet what joy it is to sing.
> In hours of toil it gives me zest,
> And when at eve I long for rest;
> When cows come home along the bars,
>   And in the fold I hear the bell,
> As Night, the shepherd, herds his stars,
>   I sing my song and all is well.

Sometimes the sun, unkindly hot,
My garden makes a desert spot.
Sometimes a blight upon the tree
Takes all my fruit away from me;
And then with throes of bitter pain
Rebellious passions rise and swell;
But—life is more than fruit or grain,
And so I sing, and all is well.

"Ere Sleep Comes Down to Soothe the Weary Eyes"
used a more elaborate verse form. It immediately
attracted the attention of people of culture.

Ere sleep comes down to soothe the weary eyes,
How questioneth the soul that other soul—
The inner sense which neither cheats nor lies,
But self exposes unto self, a scroll
Full writ with all life's acts unwise or wise,
In characters indelible and known;
So, trembling with the shock of sad surprise,
The soul doth view its awful self alone,
Ere sleep comes down to soothe the weary eyes.

"Conscience and Remorse" crystallizes an experience
in vain regret; and the companion pieces, "Promise"
and "Fulfilment" are poignant in their disillusionment.
In "A Creed and Not a Creed" (later known as "Re-
ligion") the poet showed himself a humanist in re-
ligious matters, while the deeper note of the tragedy

of his own people was to be seen in "We Wear the Mask."

> We wear the mask that grins and lies,
> It hides our cheeks and shades our eyes,—
> This debt we pay to human guile;
> With torn and bleeding hearts we smile,
> And mouth with myriad subtleties.
>
> Why should the world be overwise,
> In counting all our tears and sighs?
> Nay, let them only see us, while
>   We wear the mask.
>
> We smile, but O great Christ, our cries
> To thee from tortured souls arise.
> We sing, but oh the clay is vile
> Beneath our feet, and long the mile;
> But let the world dream otherwise,
>   We wear the mask.

Some of these pieces, the "Majors" in the book, have special significance in connection with the poet's life and art. It was the "Minors," however, devoted to humor and dialect, that were to gain for him the widest recognition; and the dialect was not only that of the Southern Negro peasant but also that of the Hoosier of the Middle West. "When Malindy Sings," with limpid rhythm, was sustained in its key in a way that denoted genius. The poem is thought to have been suggested by the singing of the author's mother, the name *Malindy* being substituted for *Matilda*. "The Party," with its high spirits and sensuous joy, "The Rivals," with its broad humor, and "When de Co'n Pone's Hot," with the rapid movement of its twelve-line stanza, were all irresistible. If Dunbar had never written another book and had passed from the scene after the appearance of *Majors and Minors*, he would still be the foremost Negro poet in the nation's literature.

After all, however, the book had been printed rather than formally published; there was no regular publicity, and the only way by which it could be sold was personal solicitation. It was for this part of the work that Dunbar, like many another author, felt that he had no special fitness. His sensitive spirit shrank from asking people to buy his wares, and sometimes he was quite discouraged. One night, after an unusually hard day, he sought out Dr. Tobey in Toledo and with tears in his eyes said he could never again offer a book to any man. Why not make up a speech? his friend suggested. He had tried that, he said, but when the time came seemed unable to say a word. "You are not a good book agent," said the doctor with a smile; and he told how that very day he had arranged for the sale of copies to three prominent men in the city on condition that the author himself call and make their acquaintance.

Dr. Tobey in fact had the zeal of a missionary in

presenting the merits of the poet he had found. One night he sat up until nearly twelve in the lobby of a hotel reading the poems with a friend. He also saw to it that a copy was left for James A. Herne, who was in the city appearing in his own play, *Shore Acres*. Mr. Herne wrote to Dunbar from Detroit, speaking enthusiastically of the poems and enclosing some pieces written by a daughter of his who was at school in Boston. He also said that he would bring the book to the attention of William Dean Howells and other literary people. Dr. Tobey meanwhile sent a copy to Colonel Robert G. Ingersoll, who was destined to have distinct influence on the poet's life.

True to his word, Mr. Herne sent his copy of the book to Mr. Howells, and that distinguished critic wrote a review of nearly a page in his regular discussion of "Life and Letters" in *Harper's Weekly*.

The issue was that reporting the nomination of William McKinley for the presidency, and tens of thousands of copies were circulated throughout the country. The date was June 27, 1896, the poet's birthday.

Told of the article by a friend, Dunbar, overwhelmed by emotion, hastened to a newsstand to get a copy.

He was just twenty-four, the age at which Byron produced *Childe Harold's Pilgrimage*.

Like the earlier poet, he awoke one morning and found himself famous.

IV

Success

Aside from any effect it may have had on the personal fortunes of Dunbar, the review by Howells is important as laying down the line that criticism was to take in later years—a line slavishly adhered to by reviewers and one about which the poet himself was not always enthusiastic. Some portions of the article would not be approved by present taste. In general, however, it was intended to be kind, and so it impressed people at the time it appeared.

"I do not remember," said the critic, "any English-speaking Negro, at least, who has till now done in verse work of at all the same moment as Paul Laurence Dunbar. . . . Burns has long had the consecration of the world's love and honor, and I shall not do this unknown but not ungifted poet the injury of comparing him with Burns; yet I do not think one can read his Negro pieces without feeling that they are of like impulse and inspiration with the work of Burns when he was most Burns, when he was most Scotch, when he was most peasant. When Burns was least himself he wrote literary English, and Mr. Dunbar writes literary English when he is least himself. But not to urge the mischievous parallel further, he is a real poet whether he speaks a dialect or whether he writes a language." After referring to the Majors and quoting "Conscience and Remorse" as representative of these, Howells continued: "Most of these pieces, however, are like most of the pieces of most young poets, cries of passionate aspiration and disappointment, more or less personal or universal, which except for the Negro face of the author one could not find specially notable. It is when we come to Mr. Dunbar's Minors that we find ourselves in the presence of a man with a direct and fresh authority to do the kind of thing he is doing." Quoting "When de Co'n Pone's Hot," "When Malindy Sings," "Accountability," and a portion of "The Party" before he concluded, he said, "I am speaking of him as a black poet, when I should be speaking of him as a poet; but the notion of what he is insists too strongly for present impartiality. I hope I have not praised him too much, because he has surprised me so very much; for his excellences are positive and not comparative. If his Minors had been written by a white man, I should have been struck by their very uncommon quality; I should have said that they were wonderful divinations. But since they are the expressions of a race-life from within the race, they seem to me infinitely more valuable and significant. . . . God hath made of one blood all nations of men: perhaps the proof of this saying is to appear in the arts, and our hostilities and prejudices are to vanish in them."

The response to this review was immediate. At the close of the article the critic referred to the printers, Hadley and Hadley, and within a few days orders for copies of the book were pouring into their office. About the same time Dunbar and his mother had occasion to be away from home for a few days, and when they returned and opened the front window, through the shutters of which the postman had thrust the mail in their absence, not less than two hundred letters were showered upon them. Meanwhile James Lane Allen, the popular novelist of Kentucky, called the attention of several editors to the work of the young poet; and thus within a few days he became a part of contemporary American letters.

On July 4, Dr. Tobey had invited Dunbar and his mother to come to Toledo, and for the reading at the hospital he had present not less than sixty guests, among whom were several of distinction. Mrs. Dunbar had no desire to go downstairs to meet the brilliant company, and it was only after much persuasion that Dr. and Mrs. Tobey prevailed upon her to be present at the recital. "It has all come at once, Paul," said the doctor, with his arm about his young friend's shoulders. "They all want to meet you now. Those who made fun of you are now eager to clasp your hand. This is going to be the testing day of your life. I hope you will bear your good fortune as bravely as you have met your disappointments. If so, that will indeed be a proof of greatness."

The recital was a triumph. When the company had gone, the poet sat alone in his room late at night thinking of all that had happened. His mind went back to the days on the elevator, to the time when he asked people to buy his first little book, and then to the dark days of the last two winters. He thought of how poverty had bruised his spirit, and how many who might have helped had turned away in coldness. Then he remembered the fatherly interest of Dr. Tobey, the kindness too of Mr. Thatcher, the sympathetic review by Howells, and how above all else God had enabled him to keep his soul inviolate. Gradually his musing took wing in a poem which he called "The Crisis." He spoke with high disdain of those who had bidden him bend his pride, of friends who had waited long to find that friendship still was sweet; and then, with the humility of one conscious of a great blessing, he said:

Mere human strength may stand ill-fortune's frown;
    So I prevailed, for human strength was mine;
But from the killing pow'r of great renown,
    Naught may protect me save a strength divine.

Help me, O Lord, in this my trembling cause;
I scorn men's curses, but I dread applause!

Now that the larger world was beckoning, it seemed
advisable for the poet to have a manager formally to
take charge of his appearances before the public, and
thus through correspondence between Mr. Howells
and a friend in Toledo he was brought in touch with
Major James B. Pond, head of a lecture bureau well
known at the time. Dunbar reminded his manager
that he had had no training for the stage; but Major
Pond told him that he did not need it, and, happening
to see Mr. Thatcher in New York, said to him that,
just a few evenings before, he had had the Negro poet
at his home for a reading before thirty guests and
that white artists were "not in it" with him when it
came to pleasing an audience.

Naturally one of the first things that Dunbar wished
to do on coming to the vicinity of New York was to
call upon the man to whom he owed so much, Wil-
liam Dean Howells. When he arrived at the home in
Far Rockaway and was announced, the novelist hur-
ried to the door to greet him, happy, he said, to meet
him personally. Luncheon was over, but Howells
kept his guest to tea and then they talked far into the
night. When Dunbar was leaving, the air had grown
chill and his host insisted on lending him an overcoat.
Howells afterward spoke of him as one of the "most

refined and modest" men he had ever met, and "truly a gentleman."

Mr. Thatcher went on to Narragansett Pier from New York, and he had told Dunbar to be ready to come thither if he received word. To some of his friends who were at the New Matthewson Hotel for the summer he read selections from *Majors and Minors,* and all expressed a desire to hear the author recite. Among those who made the request were several people from the South. The manager of the hotel heartily approved the plan, setting aside the ballroom and giving an orchestra for the occasion.

The evening was one of the most brilliant in the life of Paul Dunbar. Never did he appear to better advantage. One piece that he used was "The Corn-Stalk Fiddle," and when he came to the stanza giving the calls for the dance, he acted out the various figures of which he spoke. With the accompaniment of the orchestra he glided about the stage, his graceful figure in perfect tune with the music and the verse; and the audience became more and more enthusiastic. Before he left Narragansett Pier the poet was presented, at her request, to the widow of Jefferson Davis, and for her he gave some special readings.

Dunbar now contributed some prose sketches to the representative papers in New York; and a dinner was given in his honor by the staff of the *Century Magazine,* of which Richard Watson Gilder was editor. To appear in the *Century* had long been the goal of his ambitions. He began to send poems to the magazine when he was not more than fourteen years of age, but it was not until he was twenty-three that one was accepted. The story goes that after the dinner he read for his hosts a few of his poems, using with special effect "When Malindy Sings." While the company applauded, he turned suddenly to Mr. Gilder and, with a twinkle in his eye, said, "That's one you sent back." For a moment the distinguished editor was embarrassed, but he rose gallantly to the occasion. "We'll take it yet," he said. The poet said he was sorry but that it had been accepted by another magazine.

Meanwhile Major Pond had given him introductions to various New York publishers. Dodd, Mead and Company having offered the best terms, Dunbar arranged with that firm for the formal issue of a volume of his poems. Thus appeared in the same year *Lyrics of Lowly Life*, the book by which he became best known. The publishers had such faith in the appeal of the work that they offered a royalty advance of four hundred dollars, and this money the author used in cancelling his most pressing obligations.

Lyrics of Lowly Life was a beautiful little volume. Its advantage over the earlier books was twofold. It was in attractive form and, having a regular imprint, made the work of the author generally accessible. In the main it was a selection of the best things that had appeared in *Oak and Ivy* and *Majors and Minors;* it could hardly be called a revision of these earlier works, for, unlike some meticulous poets such as Tennyson and Poe, who constantly touched up their verse, Dunbar almost never altered a poem after it was once printed. When one was written, it was written. It might be rejected for later use, or it might be approved; but if approved, it would be taken as it was; it would not be changed.

The Introduction was by Howells, and never did that critic write anything that was more quoted. In the main the appreciation followed the line of the review of *Majors and Minors*. The book, Howells said, appealed to him for reasons quite apart from the author's race, origin, and condition. The world was too old, and he himself too much of its mood to care for the work of a poet because he was black or because he had once been an elevator-boy. Art must be judged without respect to such facts, and enjoyed or endured for what it was in itself. He then said: "What struck me in reading Mr. Dunbar's poetry was what had already struck his friends in Ohio and Indiana, in Kentucky and Illinois. They had felt, as I felt, that however gifted his race had proven itself in music, in oratory, in several of the arts, here was the first instance of an American Negro who had evinced innate distinction in literature. . . . So far as I could remember, Paul Dunbar was the only man of pure African blood and of American civilization to feel the Negro life æsthetically and express it lyrically.

It seemed to me that this had come to its most modern consciousness in him, and that his brilliant and unique achievement was to have studied the American Negro objectively, and to have represented him as he found him to be, with humor, with sympathy, and yet with what the reader must instinctively feel to be entire truthfulness. I said that a race which had come to this effect in any member of it, had attained civilization in him, and I permitted myself the imaginative prophecy that the hostilities and the prejudices which had so long constrained his race were destined to vanish in the arts; that these were to be the final proof that God had made of one blood all nations of men."

The book opens with "Ere Sleep Comes Down to Soothe the Weary Eyes" and closes with "The Party." "Ione," the first poem in *Majors and Minors*, is now given less conspicuous place. The popular favorites —"The Poet and his Song," "Life," "Ode to Ethiopia," "The Corn-Stalk Fiddle," "The Rivals," "The Spellin'-Bee," "The Ol' Tunes," "When de Co'n Pone's Hot," and "When Malindy Sings"—are all here; and along with the spontaneity, the gusto, is a sureness of taste that tells of conscious art. Sometimes there was struck a deeper note, but not so often as to change the dominant tone. All in all the book was one to be enjoyed.

It was an immediate success, not less so with the poet's own people than with the general public. Three years later when he went to the South he found that several young men were making their way through school by reading his poems. For some years after its appearance the book averaged a sale of three or four thousand copies a year—a figure naturally regarded as extraordinary, for though a novel might sell much more, only rarely does a book of poems do so well.

Early in 1897 came the suggestion that Dunbar go to England under the management of a daughter of Major Pond, and, though the terms were hardly satisfactory, he thought it advisable to take advantage of this opportunity to cross the ocean. Financially the trip was disastrous, and before he was through he had to send back to the United States for money with which to return. Nevertheless there were many pleasant experiences. He appeared at several exclusive clubs and stately homes. Among the former was the Savage Club of London, at which he won the approval of a highly critical audience. Mr. and Mrs. Henry M. Stanley entertained him at tea. John Hay, the American ambassador, was kind, and arranged for a recital before a distinguished company. On one occasion when the poet used "When de Co'n Pone's Hot," one of the men present rose to explain. "I fancy," he said, "Mr. Dunbar's poem may be a bit unintelligible to those of us who have not traveled in the States. The 'co'n pone' is a peculiar American dish in which the Southern Negroes bake their cakes." The reader was too polite to make any correction.

All the while, when he was not engaged with a recital, the struggling author worked feverishly, finding in the frequent rains and the gloom of London much in accord with his mood. In his lonely lodgings he wrote not only poems and stories but also a large portion of a novel, *The Uncalled*. His more personal experience at the time he summed up in his poem, "The Garret."

> Within a London garret high,
> Above the roofs and near the sky,
> My ill-rewarding pen I ply
>   To win me bread.
> This little chamber, six by four,
> Is castle, study, den, and more,—
> Altho' no carpet decks the floor,
>   Nor down, the bed.
>
> .   .   .   .
>
> I write my rhymes and sing away,
> And dawn may come, or dusk or day:
> Tho fare be poor, my heart is gay,
>   And full of glee.
> Though chimney-pots be all my views,
> 'Tis nearer for the winging Muse,
> So I am sure she'll not refuse
>   To visit me.

As the poet went forward with his work, he had in his thought increasing reservation about the ulti-

mate influence of what had been said by his best
known reviewer. To a friend he wrote from Lon-
don: ":One critic says a thing and the rest hasten to
say the same thing, in many cases using the identical
words. I see now very clearly that Mr. Howells has
done me irrevocable harm in the dictum he laid down
regarding my dialect verse. I am afraid that it will
even influence English criticism, although what no-
tices I have here have shown a different trend."

Back in America before the close of the summer,
Dunbar was made sharply to face the fact that rapid
toll was being taken of his strength. Numerous re-
quests came from editors for his views of things
abroad. He did not have a high regard for "impres-
sion" articles, and regretted that he was not able to
resist the demands made upon him; "but," he said to
a friend, "a golden eagle is a great corrector of the
artistic sense." One of the best of his articles thus
written was "England as Seen by a Black Man," in
the *Independent* for September 16. The thing that
the poet recalled most vividly was the dignity of Eng-
lish family life. Nothing seemed to him better to
account for the greatness of the nation than the sight
of a cultured father and mother surrounded by their
sons and daughters. The attitude of the youth to-
ward his parents, he said, interpreted Balaklava; and
for his own people he could wish nothing better than
a similarly elevated ideal of the home. There was

also a lesson for a striving, struggling people in the
general peace and contentment of English life.

Even while Dunbar was abroad he received from
Colonel Ingersoll a letter saying that it seemed pos-
sible that a position might be secured for him at the
Library of Congress in Washington. The plan ma-
terialized as soon as the poet returned to the country;
and on October 1, 1897, he began work as an assistant
in the reading room at a salary of $720 a year. The
Negro people of the country did not feel that the po-
sition was one commensurate with the talent and
achievement of their poet. He, however, had learned
only too well what it meant to be without regular
employment; so he decided to hold the place for a
while at least. He remained at the Library for fifteen
months, until the end of 1898, by which time his writ-
ing was better able to support him. Naturally to one
of his temperament it was not congenial to be con-
fined sometimes for hours in the stacks with scientific
works. In the torrid days of midsummer the iron
gratings seemed to him like the bars of a prison, es-
pecially when he came out and looked upon the invit-
ing green of the Capitol grounds. Thus it was that
he wrote "Sympathy" ("I know what the caged bird
feels, alas!").

In the earlier months of this period of library serv-
ice, that is, for the latter weeks of 1897 and for some
time in the new year, Dunbar was a guest in the home
of Professor Kelly Miller, of Howard University.

While there he finished the novel upon which he had been engaged. One day when he came in he asked his hostess if he could have a cup of tea. "No, Mrs. Miller," he said, "what I mean is a pot of tea. I am going to write to-night." Early in 1898 he left to go to a home which he had prepared for himself and his mother at 1934 Fourth Street, just a few blocks away. Before going, however, he gave to the very young son of the family a copy of *Oak and Ivy*, on the flyleaf of which he wrote an inscription, dated January 1, 1898. This is so thoroughly typical of his taste and temper that it is given herewith:

> Dear Kelly, when I was a kid
> I wrote this book: that's what I did.
> When you grow up—I may be dead—
> You allus think o' what I said,
> Dat you gon' mek yo' ma'k fu' true,
> Cos, Kelly M—, I bets on you.

The spring of 1898 was otherwise notable. As early as 1895 Dunbar had been attracted by a poem that he found in a magazine published in Boston, and even more had he been interested in the picture of the author, Alice Ruth Moore, which accompanied it. Not knowing her address, he wrote to Miss Moore in care of the magazine, enclosing the poem "Phyllis" dedicated to her picture; and the letter was forwarded to New Orleans, where she was just beginning her career as a teacher. The correspondence thus begun was continued for two years before the poets met; and in the meantime appeared *Majors and Minors* and *Lyrics of Lowly Life*, both of which volumes contained not only "Phyllis" but another poem entitled "Alice." Within this interval also Miss Moore went north to Boston to live. On the eve of Dunbar's sailing for England early in 1897, a mutual friend, Mrs. Victoria Earle Matthews, tendered him a reception in New York; and many prominent persons were present, among them Booker T. Washington. Miss Moore had been urged to come from Boston, and she now met Dunbar for the first time. They became engaged that night, and he sailed the next day. There was no time to buy a ring, but the poet slipped off his finger a little gold band that had belonged to his mother, and this was later used at his marriage. Miss Moore did not return to Boston, where she had been preparing to enter Wellesley College, but remained in New York, and within a month had taken a position as a teacher in the schools of Brooklyn. When, then, Dunbar had returned from England and found his prospects brightening, he naturally thought of having his own home. The marriage took place in New York on March 6, 1898, Bishop W. B. Derrick, of the A. M. E. Church, performing the ceremony.* The novel, *The Uncalled*, and the next volume of poems, *Lyrics of the Hearthside*, were dedicated to "Alice."

* See note, pp. 150-51.

It was very soon after his marriage that Dunbar was on the program of a meeting in New York at which the higher education of the Negro was discussed. In the audience was a man from Albany who spoke favorably of the poet to Mrs. Merrill, a patron of art and letters in that city. Even before Dunbar returned home there came to his Washington address a telegram asking terms for a recital. Regularly the fee was fifty dollars, but this time his wife, who received the message and who sensed its importance and urgency, was moved to say one hundred and expenses. The terms were accepted and a date fixed; and the recital itself was all that was expected or hoped for. In connection with it, however, the poet had to undergo one of the numerous experiences into which his unique position thrust him. Arriving at Albany about six o'clock in the evening, he asked the Negro bus driver of the Kenmore Hotel to take him there. The driver asked if he was going there to work. "No, to stay," was the reply, which was met by a grunt. At the desk of the hotel Dunbar took up the pen to register. "Hold on, there," said the clerk, "what are you going to do?" "To register of course." "You can't register here," said the clerk; "we have no rooms for you in this hotel." "Oh, yes, you have," was the reply; "a reservation has been made for me. I am Paul Laurence Dunbar." The clerk, on looking into the reservations, found it was true that one of the wealthiest women in the city had engaged the most expensive

suite for the poet, without reference to race or color.
He went to speak to the manager about the situation.
Looking Dunbar up and down the manager said, "This
Negro is crazy; telephone to the police station and let
them come up and get him." And the matter was
not adjusted until Mrs. Merrill herself appeared on the
scene and insisted on all possible courtesy for her
guest.

This was not the only experience of this sort that
Dunbar had, and only those who have felt the sting of
American prejudice can know what he sometimes suf-
fered. It might have been well if those who criticized
an occasional note of bitterness in his work could
sometimes have been in his place.

The Uncalled was accepted by *Lippincott's* and ap-
peared complete in the issue of that magazine for May,
1898. In the same year it was published in book form.
Like two others of the novels, it is concerned mainly
with white rather than Negro characters. Just why
this should be so will call for consideration in connec-
tion with Dunbar's theories of life and art. The
story of an orphan boy in an Ohio town, the child of
worthless parents, who was adopted by a prim and
strong-minded maiden lady, and by her prepared for
the ministry against his own convictions, is only partly
a success; and reviewers were quick to point out the
difficulty of making a novel revolve so largely around
one character. They also took note of the lack of
local color and the mediocre quality of the English.

The element of romance is introduced only near the close, and even then seems somewhat forced. Occasionally one catches an echo of George Eliot, as if the author, with only limited acquaintance with the novel, remembered primarily such a high school classic as *Silas Marner*. The book has significance in his life in that it represents his own pondering of the work of the ministry. Fred Brent, who at length freed himself from the calling he did not like, was to some extent Dunbar himself. All told, however, *The Uncalled* did not add to the writer's reputation.

Very different was the reception accorded *Folks from Dixie*, a collection of stories appearing in the same year. With these there was no question that the author was on familiar ground. The twelve stories, most of which had appeared in the old *Cosmopolitan*, ranged all the way from those set "befo' de war" to those dealing with the current problems of the Negro, with emphasis primarily upon the former. These naturally awakened comparison with the work of Ruth McEnery Stuart, Grace King, Joel Chandler Harris, Thomas Nelson Page, F. Hopkinson Smith, and other writers who were using material from the old South; and it was readily granted that Dunbar showed a more intuitive sense of the Negro than these authors. When, however, there was comparison with Charles W. Chesnutt, the advantage could hardly be said to be in his favor. He had an eye for the picturesque, but he was not always a deeply sympathetic observer, and in general followed the trend of the day. Of Mr. Chesnutt's deeper feeling, powerful climaxes, and finished technique he hardly seemed to be the master; nor in a large way was he helped by the grotesque illustrations by E. W. Kemble. "The Colonel's Awakening" is concerned with the faithfulness of two retainers to their old master, whose thoughts were wholly of the past. "A Family Feud" shows how an old servant could reconcile two families at war with each other. "Anner 'Lizer's Stumbling Block" is broad comedy; the heroine can not "get religion" until she knows whether Sam intends to marry her or not. "The Trial Sermons on Bull-Skin" revolves about the plan of one sister to break up the service conducted by the preacher whom she does not want to see called to the church. "Aunt Mandy's Investment" shows how a Negro confidence man seizes without compunction the funds of an investment company, but is not able to betray the faith of one old mother who is devoted to her sick son. "Jimsella" is shorter than most of the stories, but technically better; in fact, all things considered, it is perhaps the most satisfying story Dunbar ever wrote. A shiftless young Negro and his wife are living in the North and not doing well; but a little baby girl comes into the family and the father's manhood is awakened. "The Ordeal at Mt. Hope" is good in its portrayal of life in a backward Southern community. Its theme is that of industrial education; and one becomes personally interested in Howard Dokesbury, the young minister from the North, who can make no headway until he arouses in Lias, the son of the family with which he stays, the desire to make the most of things within his grasp. "At Shaft 11" has a forward look in that it takes a provocative subject, that of the Negro as a strike-breaker in a mine in West Virginia; but with a theme that called for hard and truthful realism, the author became uncertain as he advanced and he closed with a sentimental note. Even when dealing with the problem of labor he could not free himself from the old romanticism. In general *Folks from Dixie* pleased the reviewers and was a successful publishing venture. The author was working as a practical craftsman, and he knew what would be approved by the editors of the day and what would not. If one regards the collection, however, strictly in the light of the short story as a literary form, he must have reservations; and still more if he leaves the realm of art and considers the work in its bearing on the Negro in the American body politic.

While these books were appearing the young author and his wife were entering more and more into the literary and social life of the capital, Dunbar himself frequently being introduced as the "poet laureate" of his race. He joined the Bachelor-Benedict Club, and delighted in having late suppers with a few friends, after which, when the mood was on him, he would give a "war dance" for their entertainment. He also became a member of the Pen and Pencil Club, his certificate saying that "having been recommended as being a trustworthy and law-abiding citizen of the United States of America, and his ability, conduct, and his capacity having been satisfactorily commended and vouched for," he was duly commissioned as a "Colonel in the Ancient, Honorable, and Patriotic Army of Office Holders and Office Seekers." On January 3, 1899, just three days after he resigned his work at the Library, he was one of the speakers at a banquet in honor of Representative George H. White, of North Carolina. A few weeks later, at Dr. Washington's insistence, he attended at Tuskegee the annual conference of Negro farmers, which he reported for the Philadelphia *Press*. On his way thither he read at various schools and colleges, one of the most brilliant occasions being that at Spelman in Atlanta. He also wrote the school song for Tuskegee Institute, having in mind the tune used with "Fair Harvard." On February 12, in New York, he assisted in an entertainment at the Waldorf-Astoria for the benefit of Hampton Institute. The Hampton quartet sang, and others who took part were Harry T. Burleigh, baritone, and Charles Winter Wood, reader. On March 21, at the Hollis Street Theatre in Boston, he gave readings at a great meeting in behalf of Tuskegee Institute, Dr. Washington and Dr. W. E. Burghardt DuBois also appearing on the program.

The literary fruitage of these crowded years was

Lyrics of the Hearthside, which appeared in February, 1899. This was the second volume of Dunbar's poems to be issued by his New York publisher; it was his first collection since *Lyrics of Lowly Life;* and it fully maintained the standard of its predecessor. The spontaneity of the earlier volume may have been missing, but there was a deeper note, as if, amid all the acclaim, the author felt the power of a noble love, and more need of the divine. There was also a broader outlook, reflecting travel and acquaintance with the world. One could observe too a refinement in technique, and, as the title would indicate, more suggestion of the fireside. The theme is found in some lines in "On the Sea Wall":

> The waves still sing the same old song
>   That knew an elder time;
> The breakers' beat is not more strong,
>   Their music more sublime;
> And poets thro' the ages long
>   Have set these notes to rhyme.
>
> But this shall not deter my lyre,
>   Nor check my simple strain;
> If I have not the old-time fire,
>   I know the ancient pain;
> The hurt of unfulfilled desire,—
>   The ember quenched by rain.

The opening poem, "Love's Apotheosis," is a superb achievement, passionate and as finely chiselled as an exquisite piece of sculpture. "The Mystic Sea" and "A Sailor's Song" as well as "On the Sea Wall" suggest the moods of the ocean, and "Love" shows the mastery of the sonnet that the poet has now gained. From the life and scenes about him come numerous hints and promptings; thus, just around the corner from his Fourth Street residence, on Spruce Street (now U), was an arc-light that filtered through the maples, and this gave him the "shadder-mekin' trees" of "Lover's Lane." One finds here too several of the popular favorites among the author's dialect poems— "Little Brown Baby," "Angelina," "Whistling Sam," "How Lucy Backslid," and the little masterpiece, "At Candle-Lightin' Time." "Whistling Sam," we are told, disturbed the whole household while it was being composed. Everybody had to whistle the tunes, and then a musician had to come and play them on the piano, and transcribe the notation to be sure there were no mistakes. Several pieces have autobiographical significance, especially "A Death Song" and "When All is Done."

When all is done, say not my day is o'er
And that thro' night I seek a dimmer shore:
Say rather that my morn has just begun,—
I greet the dawn and not a setting sun,
　　When all is done.

Lyrics of the Hearthside enhanced Dunbar's reputation. Later in the year the book was followed by the first of the specially illustrated volumes, *Poems of Cabin and Field*, the reception of which was so cordial as to lead to several successors. About this time Dunbar also thought of writing a novel very different from much of his work, one about the Negro of education and culture. This hope he was not destined to realize. At any rate, however, in the early weeks of 1899 he was rapidly rising to the highest point in his career. Just what was he like, one may now ask, in the full flush of success? What impression did he make on those who knew him best?

In height he was slightly above the average (five feet, nine and a half inches), and his lithe figure, a little slender, seemed perfectly proportioned. His voice was of unusual quality. Some found in it a suggestion of harshness, but to most people it was resonant and mellow. The poet knew instinctively how to use it, and his eyes flashed brightly when he entered upon a reading. He appeared to special advantage in morning dress, and his ease and humor had the charm of urbanity. Mrs. Mary Church Terrell, who was for some time a next-door neighbor, has said: "Mr. Dunbar was a man of charming personality, with a bold, warm, buoyant humor of character which manifested itself delightfully to his friends. Mingled with his affability of manner were a dignity and poise of bearing which prevented the overbold from coming too near. While there was nothing intrusive or forward about Paul Dunbar, when he found himself among eminent scholars or distinguished people in the highest social circles, he showed both by his manner and his conversation that he felt he was just exactly where he was entitled to be. There was nothing that smacked of truckling, and nobody in the wildest flight of imagination could dream that Paul Dunbar felt particularly flattered at the attention he received. The maturity of intellectual power was manifested in his conversation as well as in his writing, and his fund of information was remarkable."

In his character the chief note was sincerity, and this was dominant whether the discussion was one of race, religion, or ideals of art. He would not approve fulsomeness in others any more than he desired it for himself. As has been said, he lived at a time when his people were passing through one of the most crucial periods in their history in America. By nature he was gentle, with a keen sense of the comedy of life; but the terrible events of which he read daily— the burning of the home, and the death of a Negro postmaster in South Carolina; the election troubles in that state and in Wilmington, N. C., in 1898; a gruesome lynching in Georgia, and a riot in New York— tended to harden him; and the result was something that seemed to be pessimism but that in its deeper current was a restlessness that was to tell in a later day. When he visited Boston in 1899 the poet found his

thought constantly turning to those who in other years
had labored for freedom, and thus it was that he wrote
such poems as those on Lincoln and Harriet Beecher
Stowe.   In the annals of the nation there was no more
thrilling story than that of Robert Gould Shaw, the
gallant young soldier, only son of one of the best
families in New England, who gave his life at Fort
Wagner.   Dunbar, thinking of the costliness of the
sacrifice, of all that Harvard had meant to the country,
and of the tales of injustice borne on every wind,
startled the country by contributing to the *Atlantic*
(October, 1900) the following sonnet:

Why was it that the thunder voice of Fate
   Should call thee, studious, from the classic groves,
   Where calm-eyed Pallas with still footstep roves,
And charge thee seek the turmoil of the state?
What bade thee hear the voice and rise elate,
   Leave home and kindred and thy spicy loaves,
   To lead th' unlettered and despised droves
To manhood's home and thunder at the gate?
Far better the slow blaze of Learning's light,
   The cool and quiet of her dearer fane,
Than this hot terror of a hopeless fight,
   This cold endurance of the final pain,—
Since thou and those who with thee died for right
   Have died, the Present teaches, but in vain!

The frankness and sincerity that characterized the
poet in racial matters were also to be seen when he

turned to religion. His theology was one of human-
ism; he had little sympathy with dogma, and hated
hypocrisy. At the close of *The Uncalled* Fred Brent
says to Eliphalet Hodges: "I shall do all the good I
can, Uncle 'Liph, but I shall do it in the name of poor
humanity until I come nearer to Him." When
Hodges suggests that he has lost his religion Brent
replies, "Lost it all? Uncle 'Liph, I've just come to
know what religion is. It's to be bigger and broader
and kinder, and to live and to love and be happy, so
that people around you will be happy." That was
really Paul Laurence Dunbar speaking, and he said
much the same thing in his poem "Religion." Later
he scourged "the rabid agitator who goes about the
land preaching the independence and glory of his
race, and by his very mouthings retarding both," "the
man of the cloth who thunders against the sins of the
world and from whom honest women draw away their
skirts," "the man who talks temperance and tipples
highballs"; and as to the minister addressing his people
he said: "If he is telling them all of the glory of heaven
and not showing them any of the possibilities of the
glory of earth, he is in no sense of the word a min-
ister, and he is failing of his duty. If he is attempting
to bolster up an ignorant faith with noise, bluster, and
frantic enthusiasm, he is much less a man of God than
a mountebank. There is no longer the excuse of
ignorance to be urged for these preachers and exhort-
ers. The majority of the old school, sincere in its

blunders and imperfections, has died out, and when the black preacher misleads his congregation to-day he does it wilfully." *

Dunbar's conception of his art was based on his theory of life. He felt that he was first of all a man, then an American, and incidentally a Negro. To a world that looked upon him primarily as a Negro and wanted to hear from him simply in his capacity as a Negro, he was thus a little difficult to understand. He never regarded the dialect poems as his best work, and, as he said in the eight lines entitled "The Poet," when one tried to sing of the greatest themes in life, it was hard to have the world praise only "a jingle in a broken tongue." His position was debatable, of course, but that was the way he felt. At the meeting at the Waldorf-Astoria a reporter asked about the quality of the poetry written by Negroes as compared with that of white people. Dunbar replied, "The predominating power of the African race is lyric. In that I should expect the writers of my race to excel. But, broadly speaking, their poetry will not be exotic or differ much from that of the whites. . . . For two hundred and fifty years the environment of the Negro has been American, in every respect the same as that

* See "Representative American Negroes of To-day" in The Negro Problem, New York, 1903, and "The Negro as an Individual" in Chicago Tribune, October 12, 1902.

of all other Americans." "But isn't there," continued the interviewer, "a certain tropic warmth, a cast of temperament that belongs of right to the African race?" "Ah," said the poet, "what you speak of is going to be a loss. It is inevitable. We must write like the white men. I do not mean imitate them; but our life is now the same." Then he added: "I hope you are not one of those who would hold the Negro down to a certain kind of poetry—dialect and concerning only scenes on plantations in the South?"

To a later school of Negro writers, one more definitely conscious of race, Dunbar thus appears as somewhat artificial. The difference is that wrought by the World War. About the close of that conflict Marcus Garvey, by a positively radical program, made black a fashionable color. It was something not to be apologized for, but exploited. Thenceforth one heard much about "the new Negro," and for a while Harlem was a literary capital. In Dunbar's time, however, black was not fashionable. The burden still rested upon the Negro to prove that he could do what any other man could do, and in America that meant to use the white man's technique and meet the white man's standard of excellence. It was to this task that Dunbar addressed himself. This was the test that he felt he had to satisfy, and not many will doubt that he met it admirably.

V

A Vain Quest

Just after the meeting in Boston in March, 1899, Dunbar wrote to a friend: "My readings here have been successful, the one at the Hollis Street Theatre being quite a triumph. But they have been a little too much for me, and I am now suffering from a cold, fatigue, and a bad throat." From that cold he was destined never to be free.

Within a few weeks, however, he was somewhat better, and in Lexington, Ky., he gave a recital that was one of the best of his life. He then turned his attention to Albany, N. Y., where on May 1 he was to appear in Jermain Hall. Elaborate preparations were made for the event. A distinguished company was expected to be present, and it was understood that Governor Theodore Roosevelt would introduce the poet. By the time he reached New York, however,

Dunbar was seriously ill. Pneumonia had set in, and for weeks his life hung in the balance. Both his wife and his mother were with him, and to his temporary lodgings, high above the ground, came many callers and tokens of esteem. William Dean Howells toiled up the stairs to ask about him, and Bishop Potter sent baskets of delicacies. While he was getting better, word came from Atlanta University that that institution had conferred on him the degree of Master of Arts.

After this trying experience Dunbar was never again a strong man. Some of the disturbing effects of his illness he concealed from his family and friends, and sometimes he turned to stimulants in the hope of strengthening himself. For several weeks he was in the Catskills in the effort to recuperate, but all the while he drove himself with relentless fury, turning out poems, articles, and stories in rapid succession. The close of the summer found him not materially better, and the physicians then advised that he go to Colorado. Thus it was that early in September, with his wife and his mother, he started upon the long journey across the country. At Chicago he received a telegram from the *Denver Post,* and as soon as he got to Colorado two representatives of that paper called to see him and to ask that he travel over the state and give his impressions of it. He was assured that his wife could go with him and that they would have every convenience possible. This generous offer he felt forced to decline, but it serves to show how his reputation had preceded him.

The early days of October found the family comfortably settled in a sunny little house in Harmon, a small town near Denver. Under date January 28, 1900, Dunbar wrote to Edward F. Arnold in Washington saying that the winter had been soft and pleasant and that he had spent much time out of doors. He spoke of the recent coming of Sissieretta Jones, the distinguished singer, and Booker T. Washington; then he continued: "I still have hopes of coming East in the spring, but the doctors discourage me about its being a permanent stay there; so I shall probably stop but a short time in Washington and go thence to the Catskills. . . . I am not so well now as I was at first, though my breath is somewhat better and I can read. I have given one [reading] already and am to give another one on Tuesday night."

Prominent among those who came to see the poet in his retreat was a young business man of Denver, Major William Cooke Daniels. This new friend, passionately devoted to literature, was greatly stimulated by the presence of a successful and noted author, and would ride out almost every day to see him, or would send out his carriage so that Dunbar might come to his palatial home in the city. Dunbar reveled in his magnificent library, but, keenly sensitive about being patronized, and not realizing it was he who had most to bestow, felt that it might be wise to terminate the

acquaintance.   However, he dedicated to Major Dan-
iels the new book on which he was working.

Before that book appeared, however, and in April,
just before he left for the East, there came from the
press the second of his collections of stories, *The
Strength of Gideon and Other Stories*. This, like
the first collection, was illustrated by E. W. Kemble.
The title story is set on a Southern plantation at the
time of the Civil War, and tells of a Negro who had
promised his master to stay at the place at all hazards
and care for the women, and who resisted every in-
ducement to leave as the war advanced, even the plea
of the young woman he loved that he make his way
to freedom.   "Viney's Free Papers" is in similar vein,
telling of a young slave woman who, through her
husband's industry, tasted freedom, but who, when the
test came, burned the papers rather than leave him.
Not all of the stories look thus to the past.   "The
Ingrate" was founded to some extent upon the ex-
perience of Joshua Dunbar during the Civil War.   "A
Council of State," with satirical suggestion, deals with
present-day political maneuvering, and "The Tragedy
of Three Forks" is concerned with the problem of
lynching.   Some of the shorter pieces have irresistible
humor, one of the best being "The Case of Ca'line,"
"a kitchen monologue."   Ca'line, taken to task by
the lady of the house for some of her shortcomings,
becomes intrepid in her defense.   "Now, Miss Ma'tin,"

she says, "I jes' want to show you dat I cooked dat steak an' dem 'taters the same lengt' o' time. Seems to me dey ought to be done de same." Again: "W'y, de las' fambly dat I lived wid—dat uz ol' Jedge Johnson— he said my fried food stayed by him longer than anything he evah e't." It is not difficult to see why *The Strength of Gideon* succeeded with the public.

The Love of Landry, a short novel, the fruit of the Colorado sojourn, appeared in October. The plot is slight, and, like that of *The Uncalled*, is concerned with characters who are quite apart from the life of the Negro. Mildred Osborne, a young woman of New York, is sent to Colorado by her physician; and thither she goes with her father. Landry, a young man from the East who has had some unpleasant experiences at home, seeks refreshment on the plains of the West, assuming the rôle of a cow-puncher. He falls in love with Mildred and she treats him as an inferior, not knowing that he is Landry Thayer, scion of a wealthy family in Philadelphia. He takes the condescension with good humor, saves Mildred in a moment of danger, and in the end all turns out happily. The dialogue is sometimes stilted, but the descriptions are often good, especially those of western scenes and a cattle stampede; and one passage, inserted when Mildred is about to reach Denver, is so poignant in relation to the author that it must ever make special appeal.

With all the faith one may have in one's self, with all the strong hopefulness of youth, it is yet a terrible thing to be forced away from home, from all one loves, to an unknown, uncared-for country, there to fight, hand to hand with death, an uncertain fight. There is none of the rush and clamour of battle that keeps up the soldier's courage. There is no clang of the instruments of war. The panting warrior hears no loud huzzas, and yet the deadly combat goes on; in the still night, when all the world's asleep, in the grey day, in the pale morning, it goes on, and no one knows it save himself and death. Then if he go down, he knows no hero's honors; if he win, he has no special praise. And yet, it is a terrible lone, still fight.

On his way homeward, on a Monday night early in May, Dunbar was honored by a reception in Quinn Chapel in Chicago. In the following autumn, however, occurred one of the saddest incidents of his life. On October 19, largely through the interest of Professor P. M. Pearson of Northwestern University, he was scheduled to give a reading in Evanston. The event had been well advertised and it was expected that a large audience from the University and the city would be present. Just a few days before the recital, at his home in Washington, Dunbar had had a recurrence of his illness, and a hemorrhage. Again he resorted to stimulants. When the time for the reading

came, he had not yet appeared, and he did not come
until the audience had waited half an hour.   He mum-
bled over the first one or two numbers, and repeated
one, so that at length the word passed around that he
was intoxicated.   Many of the people rose and left.
The matter was featured in the newspapers of Chi-
cago, naturally to the poet's great embarrassment, and
thenceforth, knowing he could not stand the strain,
he gave fewer and fewer readings.

This incident brings up something that was more
than once mentioned to Dunbar's discredit in the few
years he had yet to live—the matter of his drinking.
This is especially to be accounted for by the state of
his health and his manner of composition.   We have
already seen that after his serious illness in the spring of
1899 he more and more often resorted to artificial
means to spur himself to his best effort.   He was at
the height of his fame; commissions and contracts were
pouring in upon him; he frequently worked under
tremendous pressure.   What was quite as important,
however, was his habit after a heavy task was done.
In the reaction from the strain of the sustained effort
to which he had been subjected, he frequently at-
tempted nothing for days; and it was in such intervals,
when he felt physically exhausted, that he would some-
times drink heavily.   Except in such periods as these
the matter had little bearing upon his work.

In the late autumn of the year 1900, in New York,
Dunbar was in close touch with some prominent

Negro stage folk with whom he first became acquainted two or three years before. At this time attention was first being directed in a large way to Negro effort in musical comedy, and Ernest Hogan was popular as a comedian. With his gusto and unctuousness he made a strong impression on the poet. For his old friend, Richard B. Harrison, Dunbar wrote in prose two little plays (as yet unpublished), *Robert Herrick* and *Winter Roses*. The first is a light, airy drama in three acts based on the life of the English poet of the name, and is on the order of the early Robin Hood plays. The second uses the theme of an old man who was urged by his son to see his sweetheart, the daughter of a widow, and who, going to call on the maiden, found that her mother was his own first love years before. The result was such as to make everybody happy. The old man sent to the sweetheart of his youth some flowers for Christmas, calling them "winter roses."

Dunbar also wrote various lyrics and sketches to be set to music by the popular composer, Will Marion Cook. Representative of the sketches is a little one-act piece entitled *Uncle Eph's Christmas*, which was intended for use by Hogan and has in the author's work an importance far beyond what its inherent merit would suggest. While it does not go far enough to indicate that Dunbar might have become a genuine dramatist, it does at least show that he had a sense of the theatrically effective. Uncle Eph and his wife,

Aunt Chloe, are with their children in their kitchen on Christmas morning. Some neighbors come in, among whom is the village gossip; and later Eph, who has gone out on an errand, returns intoxicated to his guests, one of whom is Parson Jones. There are different songs interpolated, among them "Czar of Dixie Land" and "Hot Foot Dance"; and there is the deliberate flattering of the white public so frequent in the musical comedies of the day. The diction moreover is exaggerated. Eph, Junior, asks, "Pappy, where was de possum first perskivered?" Eph, Senior, remarks, "Don't you know dere's no sich word in the dictionumgary as perskivered?" When Chloe disputes him he says, "I's got de best edjumingation." The scene closes with the inevitable cakewalk that Williams and Walker had made popular. *Uncle Eph's Christmas* and the sketches like it show how Paul Dunbar might have spent his time if he had not had a vision of higher things.

VI

Love and Sorrow

AFTER a brief stay on the Jersey coast and a sojourn in Florida early in 1901, Dunbar returned to the capital. He was now living at 321 Spruce (U) Street, not far from his former residence. "I am afraid the climate of Washington does not suit me," he said, "but there is much to hold me here. The best Negroes in the country find their way to the capital, and I have a very congenial and delightful circle of friends."

The new home was very pleasant. On the floors were Navajo rugs brought from the West, and here and there the skin of an animal stretched before an easy chair. The walls of the study were adorned with posters, some of Kemble's drawings, and the portraits of other authors. Below were bookshelves, and in a special case copies of the poet's works, and numerous autographed volumes.

In two special articles Dunbar gave his impression
of the city.   One was "Negro Life in Washington" in
Harper's Weekly (January 13, 1900) and the other
was "Negro Society in Washington" in the *Saturday
Evening Post* (December 14, 1901).   The first was
clever in its descriptions, and the second revealed
keen insight.   Both showed that the writer had the
eye of the true journalist for essentials.   A little later
Dunbar contributed a paper, "Representative Ameri-
can Negroes," to a book entitled *The Negro Problem*
and made up of articles by prominent men of the
day.   All the while he was alert to anything that
reflected the deeper life of his people.   One evening
in Washington he heard from an old Negro the story
of a nephew in Alabama who had been falsely accused
of a grave crime.   The young man had been taken
from jail by night and strung up on the limb of a
giant oak by the roadside.   In a few weeks the leaves
on the limb turned yellow and dropped off; the
bough itself withered and died while the other
branches of the tree grew and flourished.   Thence-
forth the tree was known as "The Haunted Oak."
"That is too good a story to be forgotten," said Dun-
bar; and he wrote his notable poem on the subject.
This appeared in the *Century* (December, 1900).
The poem has the wild rhythm of the old ballads and
reveals an author very different from the one who
wrote the early dialect poems.   Some reviewers won-
dered that the *Century*, known for its gentle literary

flavor, would dare to print a piece so intensely real-
istic; and the fact that it appeared shows that Mr.
Gilder, the editor, and his associates were openminded
and ever ready to consider Dunbar's best work.

Asked one day about his methods of composition,
the poet said: "I write when convenience lets me, or
the spirit moves me, my object being to do a certain
amount of work, rather than to work a certain length
of time. When I first began my career, I wrote rap-
idly, accomplishing without difficulty five thousand
words a day. Now I write slowly—oh! so slowly.
I sometimes spend three weeks on a chapter and then
am not satisfied with the result. Indeed, I have never
yet succeeded in perfectly reproducing what was in
my mind. Fortunately for the artist, however, the
public doesn't see the mental picture, and the poor
copy isn't unfavorably contrasted. Last spring, when
filling an order for a prose composition for *Lippin-
cott's Magazine*, I wrote fifty thousand words in thirty
days, but I have never recovered from the strain of it.
Indeed, my work becomes harder, rather than easier,
as I go on, simply because I am more critical of it. I
believe when an author ceases to climb, he ceases at
the same time to lift his readers up with him. Yes, I
find that my pen yields me a support. At one time I
added to my income by reading, but since my voice
has failed I have given that up almost entirely."

The work referred to as produced under great pres-
sure was *The Sport of the Gods*, which appeared in

Lippincott's in May, 1901. Meanwhile one of the firms with which Dunbar dealt valued his work so highly that for some time it sent to him each month a retaining fee simply for the privilege of having the first chance to pass upon whatever he might produce. When editors were so eager to receive his work there was only one thing that he feared, and that was that he might lose the freshness and spontaneity for which he was known, as when he received one day an order for a group of seven songs.

About the first of March, 1901, the poet received two official documents. The first was a parchment giving him the rank of Colonel for the Inaugural Parade of President McKinley, and the second designated him as an aid of the Third Civic Division. At first he refused absolutely to appear in the parade, as he did not consider himself a good horseman. His wife and his mother made siege upon him, however, and prevailed on him to change his mind. Thus it was that he appeared in the procession.

On the next New Year's Day, after Roosevelt had succeeded to the presidency, Dunbar felt an impulse to go with a friend and pay his respects to the President whom he remembered so pleasantly. The line was long, and as he waited he wondered why he had come. When at last it was his turn to shake hands and his name was given, the President greeted him with warmth, putting his hand on his shoulder and pulling him from the line, so that for a moment there was confusion. As he left the White House the author remarked to his friend that if he had known he would have made as much disturbance as that, he never would have come.

Meanwhile he himself had visitors, so many at times that it was difficult to work to advantage. His friends had to work to relieve him from those who were wearisome. One night about nine-thirty the bell rang and when the card was given to him, he saw the name of the son of one of the country's wealthiest families. The visitor said that he had to go to England two or three times a year, that he was to go again within a few days, and that on previous trips so many people had asked him if he knew Paul Laurence Dunbar that he was determined not to go again without having made the poet's acquaintance. Dunbar laughed and asked him to have a seat.

In these crowded years about the turn of the century the poet was at the very height of his achievement. He could not possibly surpass the freshness of his early work; but his reputation was now established, there was demand for whatever he wrote, and books came from the press in rapid succession. It was as if he knew that he was doomed, and that every hour of activity was so much snatched from the "eternal silence."

Suddenly came the crash, a sorrow's crown of sorrow. Early in 1902 the poet and his gifted wife separated, and the beautiful home was broken up.

There were no formal proceedings, and thenceforth each of the two was very gracious in any reference to the other. Some years after her husband's death Mrs. Dunbar married Mr. Robert J. Nelson of Philadelphia, so that she was known in her later life as Alice Dunbar Nelson.

Dunbar left Washington never to return. For a while he was in Chicago, but soon he went to Dayton, to the home he had purchased for his mother. In December he wrote to his old friend, Mr. Thatcher, of Toledo:

> My plans are few but definite. There is a midwinter book of poems forthcoming, *Lyrics of Love and Laughter,* and an illustrated one for next fall. An Ohio novel is promised to *Lippincott's,* and dialect stories and verses to various periodicals. Besides this I shall probably read in the Southwest during the latter part of January. My appearance is robust, but my cough is about as bad as it can be.

The books which represent the later Washington sojourn are six: *The Fanatics* (1901), *Candle-Lightin' Time* (1901), *The Sport of the Gods* (1902), *Lyrics of Love and Laughter* (1903), *In Old Plantation Days* (1903), and *When Malindy Sings* (1903). The two illustrated volumes, *Candle-Lightin' Time* and *When Malindy Sings,* fully maintain the standard set by

Poems of Cabin and Field; and the former contains the charming poem "Lullaby" ("Kiver up yo' haid, my little lady") which is not to be found in the complete edition of the poet's work, probably because he used the title "Lullaby" more than once. Both books serve to show the popularity of the author's work in this form. After all, however, chief interest attaches to the books representing fresh effort, and these include two novels, a collection of poems, and a collection of short stories.

The Fanatics reminds one of the short story, "At Shaft 11," in that it leaves the realm of the romantic and deals with the inflammable material of a social and political problem. All in all, however, the novel is hardly more satisfying than the shorter piece of work, and the reception it received was a great disappointment to the author, who had labored earnestly upon it. The book breaks with the past and yet only partly looks to the future. The incidents are set just before and just after the Civil War in Dorbury, a little town in Ohio, where there are strong sympathizers with the Union and also some stalwart Southerners. Bradford Waters represents the former and Stephen Van Doren the latter; and complication arises when their children, Mary Waters and Robert Van Doren, fall in love. Prominent also among the characters is Forsyth, a demagogue. There is strange antagonism to the Negroes who have made their way from the South and are coming in increasing numbers to the town.

The churches are cold, and the Negroes who have always lived in Durbury are not more friendly. "For the time all party lines fell away, and all the people were united in one cause—resistance of the black horde. It was at this time that Butler's proclamation struck through the turmoil like a thunderbolt, and the word 'contraband' became a menace to the whites and a reproach to the blacks." In the course of the story Forsyth is killed by a contraband. One can but imagine what Dunbar would have made of a novel mainly devoted to the effort of the struggling people from the South to find a new home in the North.

The Sport of the Gods is that one of the author's books about which there might naturally be the greatest debate. The story is concerned with the transplanting of a Negro family from a backward Southern community to the swifter currents of Harlem. Berry Hamilton, the father, is falsely accused and imprisoned because of a theft, and when after some years he is free, he goes to New York to find his wife married to another man, his son in the penitentiary because of a murder he has committed, and his daughter "not the girl she used to be." The first part of the story uses old material and treats it in conventional fashion. In the description of the Southern plantation and the Negroes who live on it there is little to separate this story from many others. Of the latter portion, however, the *Bookman* (April, 1906) said: "Mr. Dunbar, out of the abundance of intimate knowledge, has told us things of which we can find no mention elsewhere in our literature. He has shown us the life of those Negroes who are not day laborers, who possess varying degrees of education, and who may even be comparatively wealthy." When the book was published in England, however, under the title *The Jest of Fate*, the *Athenaeum* (November 29, 1902) took a view not nearly so favorable. It criticized the work as crude and unrestrained melodrama, the title as trite, the talk of the white gentlefolk as stilted and absurd, and the work in general as full of unpleasant suggestions and surprising colloquialisms. There is truth in both points of view. In attempting the sternly realistic portrayal of Negro life in New York in some of its more sordid phases, Dunbar was opening up a new field and one that looked to the future. It is quite as certain that he went little below the surface of his subject and that his artistry was not complete. *The Sport of the Gods* thus remains a work of promise rather than one of assured achievement. No one of the four novels of the author was an unqualified success. The question is raised accordingly whether he worked to best advantage in large form and might not better have restricted himself to poetry and the short prose sketch.

In Old Plantation Days was inscribed to the well known editor of the *Saturday Evening Post*, George Horace Lorimer, "out of whose suggestion these stories were born, and by whose kindness they first saw light." The title indicates the limitations within which the author worked. At the same time, considered simply as stories, those included in this volume are among the best Dunbar ever wrote. They are set on the plantation of Stuart Mordaunt, and one piece after another reveals good craftsmanship. "Aunt Tempy's Triumph" shows the place of a family servant of forceful character in the old régime. In the next story Aunt Tempy is seen in tenderer guise. In "The Walls of Jericho" the methods of a sensational preacher are used to his discomfiture, and "How Brother Parker Fell from Grace" shows the exhorter of the plantation also embarrassed. The stories were after a pattern, but there was little question as to practical success.

Lyrics of Love and Laughter represents the fruitage in verse of the four years since the appearance of *Lyrics of the Hearthside,* and the volume thus shows the poet at full maturity. It was addressed to Miss Catherine Impey, who with her mother and sister helped to make the visit to England a pleasant memory. While the charm of "At Candle-Lightin' Time" and the poignancy of "When All is Done" were not likely to be surpassed, the new book contained even more poems of distinction than *Lyrics of the Hearthside,* and several that had personal interest. It also reveals as few others the working of a poetic mind. "Dat Ol' Mare o' Mine" goes back to the sojourn in Colorado, where the author saw a horse of uncertain age that was very eccentric but that could come home unassisted "on de ve'y da'kes' night." "A Warm Day in Winter" and "Spring Fever" also call up the days in Harmon, while "By Rugged Ways," somewhat like "Slow Through the Dark," was suggested by a small caravan making its way up a mountain. The months in the Catskills were especially rich in suggestion. One morning through the rain the poet heard the plaintive but cheering song of a little phœbe bird, and thus we have both "Joggin Erlong" and "Keep a Song up on de Way." The whip-poor-will made a very different impression, as may be seen from "Whip-poor-will and Katy-Did." Was the cry "whip-poor-will," the poet asked, a command or a query with a plea for exoneration? To him the nervous haste, the tattling, the raucousness called up a boy who knew he was not blameless but who nevertheless tried to exonerate himself; and thus it was that the poem took a whimsical and humorous turn. In even lighter vein was "Ballade," which grew out of visits to West Medford, Mass. To the poet the Mystic River called up not so much historic associations as a desire to fish; but when he went forth with a vision of dace and bream, he was doomed, alas! to disappointment, for all about in the shady lanes were signs "To Let" and "To Sell." "Arcadia has trolley lines," he sighed as he wended his way homeward.

Where so much is good it is hard to award a palm for excellence. "Encouragement," with its line,

"Speak up, Ike, an' 'spress yourself," kept up the tradition of high spirits and broad humor set by "The Party" and "Angelina," while "In the Morning," with its address to the delinquent Lias, immediately became popular as a reading. Here also are "Two Little Boots," "Fishing," "The Colored Band," "When Dey 'Listed Colored Soldiers," "Howdy, Honey, Howdy," "The Old Front Gate," "To the Eastern Shore," "Li'l Gal," "Itching Heels," and "The Haunted Oak." A tribute is paid to Lincoln, and here are the sonnets addressed to Robert Gould Shaw, Douglass, and Booker T. Washington. "To the Road" is in the spirit of *Songs from Vagabondia*. Coming close to the heart of the poet one finds not only "To a Violet Found on All Saints' Day" but also "Weltschmertz," "The Monk's Walk," "The Poet," and "Life's Tragedy."

One poem calls for special note. "To the South," different from most of the other pieces, is amazing in the light it throws on Dunbar's approach to a social theme. If any subject could possibly arouse indignation in a Negro poet about the year 1902, one would suppose it would be the peonage and the convict lease system in the South. Instead of being dynamic, however, Dunbar sentimentalizes throughout a fairly long piece of work. He says that the time has come to strike "deeper chords, the notes of wrong"; but he appeals to the South on the basis of old memories. The verse medium is slow—the rhymed iambic pentameter. If there had been a rapid succession of lines, even this might have had such power as in Edwin Markham's "Dreyfus"; but the division is into quatrains, and the result is a distinct eighteenth-century flavor. Even the diction is pseudo-classic—"tropic sun," "midnight owl," "honored head," "joyless morn," "dangerous ease," "gladsome song"; and such a line as "For him no more the lamp shall glow at eve" takes one straight back to Gray's "Elegy." It is such a poem as this that in recent years has sometimes led to sharp reaction against Dunbar. If it were his best work, he would already have passed into oblivion. Very seldom is he so inept.

The best work in *Lyrics of Love and Laughter* is that which gives voice to infinite yearning. It is in this that a universal note is struck. At the close of the volume is a group of five little poems entitled "Lyrics of Love and Sorrow." The title might well have been that for the book. Another poem, "Life's Tragedy," is in the same temper and in the spirit of Browning's lines,

Oh, the little more, and how much it is!
    And the little less, and what worlds away!

It may be misery not to sing at all
    And to go silent through the brimming day.
It may be sorrow never to have loved,
    But deeper griefs than these beset the way.

To have come near to sing the perfect song
 And only by a half-tone lost the key,
There is the potent sorrow, there the grief,
 The pale, sad staring of life's tragedy.

To have just missed the perfect love,
 Not the hot passion of untempered youth,
But that which lays aside its vanity
 And gives thee, for thy trusting worship, truth—

This, this it is to be accursed indeed;
 For if we mortals love, or if we sing,
We count our joys not by the things we have,
 But by what kept us from the perfect thing.

Candlelight

BACK in Dayton, amid scenes that he remembered vividly, the poet resumed his tasks. He was among old friends, one of the best being Dr. William Burns, whom he had known from youth and who was his constant attendant. To the home on North Summit came also many visitors. All received the utmost courtesy. When congenial spirits gathered, there might be a tea or an impromptu musicale.

One day when some ladies were present, a young acquaintance called to take Dunbar for a drive. He could not go, not only because of his guests but also because that day he was too weak to leave the house. At the same time the man who had been so thoughtful must not be offended. Accordingly Dunbar greeted him affectionately and presented him as a "talented friend" who wrote "beautiful verses."

The study has remained in recent years very much as the poet left it. The room is the front one on the second floor. As one enters he finds on the right by the door the glass-covered case in which were kept the most precious books. Beyond on the right are open shelves, in front of which is the couch on which Dunbar would rest when tired. On the left, in the farther corner by the window, is the flat-top desk on which he worked. On it are various curios and the typewriter, while near by is the tabouret with the tea service. Near also has now been placed a bicycle presented by Dr. Tobey. Close to the door on the left wall is an autograph copy of "America" sent by a friend in Connecticut, while all about are special commissions and the pictures of friends. Two of the photographs are of Sissieretta Jones, who called when she came to Dayton to sing. Another is one of Eugene Field which Dunbar had admired and which was sent him by Mrs. Field after her husband had died. Among the books that were treasured is a copy of *In the Forest of Arden,* by Hamilton Wright Mabie, presented by the poet's publisher, Mr. Frank H. Dodd, under date February 14, 1899. There is a copy of *The Future of the American Negro,* sent with the "kind wishes of Booker T. Washington, Feb. 19, 1901." There are also autographed copies of works by Harriet Prescott Spofford, Waldo H. Dunn, and other authors; and a book that especially delighted the poet in his last illness was *The Lover's Mother Goose*, sent by John Cecil Clay.

In the autumn of 1904 Dunbar wrote for Theodore Roosevelt a campaign poem of four stanzas. The President acknowledged this as follows: "I am touched that you should have written me from your sick bed. I appreciate the poem. As a token of my regard, will you accept the accompanying two volumes of my speeches?" The two books are the *Presidential Addresses* and *State Papers* from the *Works* of the President, and the inscription reads:

> To Paul Laurence Dunbar, Esq.
> With the regards of
> Theodore Roosevelt
> Nov. 2ᵈ, 1904.

By this time the poet was thin of body and pallid in complexion, and he would sit for hours in a large chair by a window propped up by pillows, his mother all the while giving solicitous attention. To a friend he wrote: "I have been very ill and am glad to be here at home where good nursing and good air ought to do me good, but I fear that I am not going to be allowed a chance to stay, as the doctors are crying California, California, even as before they cried Colorado."

The Heart of Happy Hollow, a collection of stories and sketches, and *Li'l' Gal*, an illustrated volume, one of the best of the series, came from the press in 1904. The former volume deals with various phases of the life of the Negro, and Happy Hollow is "wherever Negroes colonise in the cities or villages, North or South . . . wherever laughter and tears rub elbows day by day, and the spirit of labour and laziness shake hands." It will thus be seen that the book has wider scope than *In Old Plantation Days;* at the same time it was generally taken as further proof that the author was not as good in prose as in poetry. "The Race Question," so aptly named, has nothing to do with sociology but is concerned with an old man who visits a race track. "The Scapegoat" deals with the turning of an election in which Negroes play an important part, while "The Boy and the Bayonet" is founded upon the high school drills which are a popular feature of life in Washington in the spring.

Lyrics of Sunshine and Shadow (1905) could not possibly equal its predecessors. The little volume is thinner in bulk than the others, and the poems, with a few notable exceptions, have not the power of several of the earlier ones. It could hardly have been otherwise. A prominent feature is the emphasis upon child life. Dunbar was always fond of children, and as the years brought increasing sorrow, they also brought more tenderness. One finds, among other things, "A Boy's Summer Song," "The Sand-Man," "Johnny Speaks," "The Plantation Child's Lullaby," "Curiosity" ("Mammy's in de kitchen, an' de do' is shet"), "Putting the Baby Away," "The Fisher Child's Lullaby," "The Farm Child's Lullaby," and "Appreciation" ("My muvver's ist the nicest one"). There are also poems of poignant sorrow. In "A Lost Dream" the author speaks of a joy that he once knew but that is no longer his. Together he and his love had fared hand in hand, and he had known the joy of her companionship. When days were bleak and winds were rude, she was by his side; and in summer, remembering the Catskills, he recalled that "the bird's call and the water's drone" and "the waterfall that sang all night" were for them alone. Now all was changed, and the dream was shattered; but how could such a dream possess him so? Above all else, however, far above all else, is the swan-song, "Compensation" (also in *Lippincott's*, December, 1905):

> Because I had loved so deeply,
>   Because I had loved so long,
> God in his great compassion
>   Gave me the gift of song.
>
> Because I have loved so vainly,
>   And sung with such faltering breath,
> The Master in infinite mercy
>   Offers the boon of Death.

Later in the year there was another illustrated volume, *Howdy, Honey, Howdy*. This was one of the most elaborate of these special publications, but the reproductions were much smaller than in the previous volumes, and the illustrations for such poems as "Encouragement" and "Angelina" hardly suggested their full flavor.*

The last birthday that Dunbar lived to see, June 27, 1905, was made a notable occasion by his friends. As Mrs. Wiggins tells the story, the poet's physician was in the plot and one afternoon gave him permission to go riding. A conspirator called with a carriage, quite innocently of course, and while Dunbar was out, the house was made ready for the party. The chair at the head of the table was festooned in purple; there was a great birthday cake; and flowers were everywhere around. When the poet returned from his drive, he walked slowly up the steps and across the veranda, totally unprepared for the sight that greeted him when he opened the door. Before long, however, his old spirit returned, and he was the gayest of all those present.

The next month the Ohio Federation of Colored

---

* Early in 1906, but after the poet had died, there appeared a similar volume, *Joggin' Erlong*. In 1907 was issued the subscription edition of the poems and stories, and this had the important addition of the biography by Mrs. Wiggins. In 1913 appeared *Complete Poems*, and in 1914 an exceptionally beautiful little book, *Speaking o' Christmas*, containing not only the Christmas poems but several others in bright vein.

Women's Clubs held its meeting in Dayton, and among the speakers was Mrs. Mary Church Terrell, who during the meetings was a guest in the Dunbar home. One day, after some charming young women had called to pay their respects to the poet, she said to him, "Sometimes I am tempted to believe you are not half so ill as you pretend to be. I believe you are just playing the rôle of interesting invalid, so as to receive the sympathy and the homage of these beautiful girls." Appreciating the pleasantry, he replied, "Sometimes I think I am just loafing myself." When Mrs. Terrell returned home, she received a copy of *Lyrics of Sunshine and Shadow* with an inscription suggesting that he was still "jes a loafin' 'roun.'"

Four months later, in November, a great blow befell him. With little warning his capable physician and friend, Dr. Burns, was struck down at the height of his powers. As ill as Dunbar was, he insisted on being taken to the home, and for some time he talked to his friend just as if he were alive. Never afterward did he seem to realize that "Bud" was really gone.

About the middle of the next month he wrote: "My life consists in going to bed at the beginning of the month and staying there, with very brief intervals of half an hour or so, until the beginning of the next month. . . . Of course there are some friends who come in, and some books that occasionally I get to read, but usually I am studying the pattern of the ceiling until I could make a very clever sketch of it from memory without the trouble of learning to draw." As late as December 30 he was still bright and said: "I am lying fallow. I believe my soil has become greatly impoverished, and it will take a good many more rains and snows to put anything into it worth coming out in blossom. But my greatest help will be the knowledge that my friends keep in touch with me, and now and then a line like an electric spark flashes from one to the other and I am new again and unafraid."

After the holidays his condition steadily became more critical.

By Friday, February 9, it could be seen that the hours that remained were not many.

Early in the afternoon a physician and then a minister came. Thrice the poet asked the time, and whether it was day or night.

The Twenty-third Psalm was read. He tried to say the words. "Through the valley of the shadow," he repeated; and then he entered into rest.

It was half-past three o'clock.

The grief of his mother was overwhelming. Messages poured into the home. "Receive my sympathy," said Mrs. Field. "Be comforted in your son's greatness."

The service was held on Monday afternoon, February 12, at the Eaker Street A. M. E. Church in Dayton. Dr. Tobey was present and he spoke out of the depth of his sorrow. He also read a letter from another close friend, Brand Whitlock, Mayor of Toledo, the grave illness of whose mother kept him from coming. "If friendship knew obligation," said Mr. Whitlock, "I would acknowledge my debt to you for the boon of knowing Paul Dunbar. It is one of the countless good deeds to your credit that you were among the first to recognize the poet in him and help him to a larger and freer life. . . . For Paul was a poet: and I find that when I have said that I have said the greatest and most splendid thing that can be said about a man. . . . The true poet is universal as is the love he incarnates in himself, and Paul's best poetry has this quality of universality."

Temporarily the body was placed in a vault. Two months later it was taken to Woodland Cemetery in Dayton.

The grave is on a slight elevation, near the road, and by it is a little willow. Just a few feet beyond is a small lake, while not far away, still closer to the road, is a giant oak.

Three years later, on the occasion of his birthday, leading citizens of Dayton paid tribute to the poet by unveiling a monument erected by popular subscription. More than a thousand were present on that beautiful morning in June. Several prominent persons came from other cities. James Whitcomb Riley was there, and the Philharmonic Society sang words of the poet set to music.

The monument was a granite boulder on the surface

of which was a bronze plate.   On the plate one may read:

PAUL LAURENCE
DUNBAR
1872   1906
"LAY ME DOWN BENEAF DE WILLERS IN DE GRASS,
WHERE DE BRANCH'LL GO A-SINGIN' AS IT PASS.
    AN' W'EN I'S A-LAYIN' LOW
    I KIN HEAH IT AS I GO,
SAYIN', 'SLEEP, MA HONEY, TEK YO' RES' AT LAS'.'"

Some years later a similar tablet was placed at the entrance to the home with the inscription:

HOME
OF
PAUL LAURENCE DUNBAR
1872   ★   1906
"BECAUSE I HAD LOVED SO DEEPLY
BECAUSE I HAD LOVED SO LONG
GOD IN HIS GREAT COMPASSION
GAVE ME A GIFT OF SONG."
ERECTED BY
BOY SCOUTS
Y. M. C. A. TROOP No. 30
JUNE 27 1921

VIII

The Poet and His Song

Paul Laurence Dunbar was unique in the literature and the life of his time. His genius commanded the attention of the great, the wise and the good; and his modesty increased their admiration. His life was a sad one, though not as incomplete as one might think. Of all the deeper striving, however, the world knew but little. What it knew was that a youth of humble birth had in a difficult field won dazzling success. The acclaim sometimes became adulation. Only the insight, the humor, and the retiring spirit of the poet enabled him to keep his soul.

In his lifetime Dunbar produced six original collections of poems, and each volume has significance for his career. *Oak and Ivy* is the effort of a youth just out of high school, and there is naturally much imitation of favorite authors, though two or three of the pieces are among the poet's best. Three years later appeared *Majors and Minors*, a work revealing deepening insight, firmer mastery of technique, and greater enrichment of spiritual experience. Some of the poems show disillusionment, but the dialect numbers run the gamut from tenderness and pathos to rollicking spirits and gusto in the enjoyment of life. Both of these early productions were handicapped by the fact that they were privately issued. Such was not the case with *Lyrics of Lowly Life*, which bore a standard imprint and included the best of what was in its predecessors. The book had beautiful form, and in general represents the tenderness and the exuberance of the poet's youth. It struck a fresh note and met with extraordinary success. After another interval of three years, marked by travel and marriage, Dunbar published *Lyrics of the Hearthside*, a mature work, with evidence of both a broader outlook and finer artistry. The dialect is still here, but the author is now moved more by a universal appeal, and the mountain, the wind, and the sea speak to him as never before. Four years later came *Lyrics of Love and Laughter*, closing with the group of poems, "Lyrics of Love and Sorrow." There is pathos, but no loss of power; and along with deep sentiment is a new emphasis on social themes. Two years later appeared *Lyrics of Sunshine and Shadow*, the thinnest of all the volumes except *Oak and Ivy*. There are several poems of childhood, but the dominant note is one of hope betrayed, and the suggestion is insistent that the wand will soon be broken.

Meanwhile the lyric quality of Dunbar's verse led several composers to set his pieces to music. No phase of his work, however, offers to the student more difficulties than this. A song is often known by its first line or a refrain rather than its formal title, and at least one or two pieces ascribed to the poet it is hard to find in any collection of his work. Among the best known songs that use his words are "On the Road," by Mark Andrews; "Who Knows?" ("A Song": Thou art the soul of a summer's day), by Ernest R. Ball; "Po' Little Lamb" ("Lullaby": Bedtime's come fu' little boys), by Carrie Jacobs Bond; "A Corn-Song" and "An Ante-Bellum Sermon," by Harry T. Burleigh; "Treat Me Nice," by John Alden Carpenter; "A Corn-Song," "How Shall I Woo Thee?" and "Over the Hills," by Samuel Coleridge-Taylor; "Jump Back, Honey" ("A Negro Love Song"), "Lover's Lane," "My Lady," and "Returned," by Will Marion Cook; "Invitation to Love," by Granville English; "Li'l' Gal," by Rosamond Johnson; "Longing," by Hazel Gertrude Kinscella; "Dawn," by Franco Leoni; "Life," by Mrs. Mary Turner Salter; "Winter's Approach," by William Grant Still; "Beyond the Years," "Invitation to Love," and "Love's Forgetfulness," by Theophil Wendt; and

"Good Night" and "Ships that Pass in the Night," by Gerald Tyler.*

The history of the poet's reputation was determined by the life of his people in the United States. At his appearance they were thrilled with hope, and about the turn of the century hardly a Negro college failed to have six or eight young men who tried to write verses like his. For a decade after he passed, there was still high esteem. Then with the war came reaction. Free verse became a popular medium, and the themes of the hour were strongly realistic, sometimes sordid or coarse. To a new school of Negro poets the dialect pieces seemed hopelessly of the past, and the poems in classic English weak and sentimental. Even discount, however, could not make Dunbar lose the heart of his people, and within more recent years there has been increasing regard, though with a shift of emphasis. To-day not only in Dayton and Washington but in about thirty other cities, high schools are named for him; in New York are the Paul Laurence Dunbar Apartments and the Dunbar Bank; and there are theatres and literary societies innumerable. It may thus not be amiss to inquire as to the basis of the

* In general the pieces by Andrews, Burleigh, Carpenter, Cook, Kinscella, Salter, Still, and Tyler have been issued by G. Schirmer, Inc. (3 East 43rd Street, New York); but "Po' Little Lamb" is issued by the Boston Music Company, "Who Knows?" by Witmark & Co., and "A Corn-Song" (Burleigh) by G. Ricordi & Co.

fame of the poet, and the place he will ultimately hold in the literature of his country and the world.

At the outset it seems necessary to save him from his friends. Just because Dunbar was unique and greatly beloved, there has sometimes been a tendency to speak of him in terms of extravagance. It has not been enough to say that he is a pleasing poet or a true interpreter of his people; there have been those who have not been satisfied to accord to him anything less than greatness. This is claiming a little too much. If, however, he is not to be placed in the highest order of poets, it might not be unreasonable for some admirer to ask, Why not? The answer to this question takes us, even if briefly, into a consideration of the nature of poetry.

As an art, poetry is primarily concerned with the expression of a sentiment or conception—not with the inculcation of truth or the appeal to duty, but with expression. Just as the sculptor realizes his vision in bronze or marble, or as the musician uses an instrument, so the poet must employ words as his medium. It is obvious of course that expression in words may be of more than one sort. Sometimes one states a fact, gives voice to an opinion, or even ventures a bit of advice. In such case it is the mind which is primarily at work, and the expression normally takes the form of prose. Sometimes, however, we wish to get away from all such matters of fact and enter the realm of fancy or sentiment. We leave the real and strive for the ideal. The imagination takes wing and we build a dream world. So doing we enter the realm of poetry.

It is also obvious, perhaps, that when we give rein to the imagination, a single word is not sufficient for the embodiment of our hope or yearning. A single word is in fact nothing more to the poet than a key on the piano is to the musician. In combination with other words, however, it may suddenly assume the highest significance, even a magical quality. It may be endlessly suggestive—the distilled quintessence of excellence. It interprets truth at the same time that it creates beauty; and it is this matter of the magic phrase that is the ultimate test of a poet. It is by this test that Shakespeare and Milton so easily establish their supremacy. It is this also that accounts for the high ranking among English poets that the critics always give to Keats and Shelley, though much that these authors wrote seems remote from common interest. Wordsworth with all his prosiness frequently meets the test and in so doing is thus saved as a great poet.

A few, only a few, illustrations must suffice. *Hamlet* is a play that is strewn with notable phrases, and so is even one of Shakespeare's less familiar productions, *Measure for Measure.* Ophelia speaks of one's treading "the primrose path of dalliance," Hamlet of holding "the mirror up to nature," and the King of "offence's gilded hand" that "shoves by justice." A whole system of theology is summed up in the phrase, "a divinity that shapes our ends," and a political faith in "such divinity doth hedge a king." In the first act of *The Tempest* Prospero is speaking to Miranda about what she recalls from her infancy. He asks,

> What seest thou else
> In the dark backward and abysm of time?

A little later he says,

> Sit still, and hear the last of our sea-sorrow.

In "Il Penseroso" Milton speaks of notes so beautiful that they "drew iron tears down Pluto's cheek." Either iron or tears may be commonplace enough; but the two words together open before us a picture of the lower regions over which Pluto presided. Keats has so many of these superb phrases in "The Eve of St. Agnes" that they seem like jewels cast lavishly over a rich carpet: "Flattered to tears," "music yearning like a god in pain," "asleep in lap of legends old," "purple riot," "hushed carpet," "perfume light," "poppied warmth of sleep," "noiseless as fear in a wide wilderness," "the sapphire heaven's deep repose." At the close of one speech in *Prometheus Unbound* Shelley uses half a dozen such conceptions in little more than so many lines. Asia is describing early morn in spring:

The point of one white star is quivering still
Deep in the orange light of widening morn
Beyond the purple mountains; through a chasm
Of wind-divided mist the darker lake
Reflects it; now it wanes; it gleams again
As the waves fade, and as the burning threads
Of woven cloud unravel in pale air;
'Tis lost! and through yon peaks of cloudlike snow
The roseate sunlight quivers; hear I not
The Aeolian music of her sea-green plumes
Winnowing the crimson dawn?

It is such effects as these that are the despair of the
minor poet, and even of many a poet otherwise excel-
lent. Two or three words in the hands of a master
open a world of beauty or give a distillation of ex-
perience. Compared with this, all ordinary rhetorical
and metrical effects seem to pale; and all poets who
depend upon such means fall short of final achieve-
ment. This applies with special force to the poets of
the United States. Not one in the nation's literature
has ever risen to the highest eminence. Longfellow
has his charm and his superb similes, Poe his brilliant
rhythm, Lowell his moral quality, Whittier his love of
nature and his high integrity, but not one of these is
a Shakespeare, a Milton, or a Keats. Whitman, who
has received exaggerated praise in recent years, is im-
portant primarily for the principles that moved him;
and Lanier was eminently a technician. Of our

greater figures, strange as it may seem, it is Bryant
and Emerson who in their best moments come nearest
to greatness; but neither of these could remain long
on a high key.

If now we ask how Dunbar answers this test of the
magic phrase, we shall see the reason for the attention
directed to the early poem, "Ere Sleep Comes Down
to Soothe the Weary Eyes." This poem was at-
tempting something in the grand manner, and it came
very near to success. The author speaks of "echoes
faint of sad and soul-sick cries,"

> And pangs of vague inexplicable pain
> That pay the spirit's ceaseless enterprise.

The first of these two lines is good (if one will be sure
to pronounce the words correctly); the second is un-
fortunately crowded with sibilants. We are trans-
ported later

> To lands unspeakable—beyond surmise,
> Where shapes unknowable to being spring.

Both of these lines are good. Unfortunately, how-
ever, they call up two of the best in Keats:

> Charm'd magic casements, opening on the foam
> Of perilous seas, in faëry lands forlorn.

If the hard test of phrasing is applied, neither in this
poem nor in any other does Dunbar reach final

achievement.   This is not necessarily to his discredit, for, as we have seen, he has some very good company.

If our poet, however, must be saved from extravagant encomium, he must also not receive undue dispraise; and this has too often been the tendency in recent years.   One of our ablest critics says: "The poetry of Dunbar is true to the life of the Negro and expresses characteristically what he felt and knew to be the temper and condition of his people.   But its moods reflect chiefly those of the era of Reconstruction and just a little beyond,—the limited experience of a transitional period, the rather helpless and subservient era of testing freedom and reaching out through the difficulties of life to the emotional compensations of laughter and tears.   It is the poetry of the happy peasant and the plaintive minstrel.   Occasionally, as in the sonnet to Robert Gould Shaw and the 'Ode to Ethiopia' there broke through Dunbar, as through the crevices of his spirit, a burning and brooding aspiration, an awakening and virile consciousness of race.   But for the most part, his dreams were anchored to the minor whimsies; his deepest poetic inspiration was sentiment.   He expressed a folk temperament, but not a race soul.   Dunbar was the end of a regime, and not the beginning of a tradition, as so many careless critics seem to think." *

* See "The Negro in American Literature," by William Stanley Braithwaite, originally in the *Crisis* and included in *The New Negro*, edited by Alain Locke.

Recently there has been another point of view. In these latter years, when capitalism has been on the defensive, there has been a tendency to study everything in its bearing on large groups of workers; and Dunbar's poetry has not escaped. Eugene Gordon, writing in *New Masses*, has said: "Paul Laurence Dunbar belonged to the Negro proletariat, but his aspirations, as he acquired friends among both the white and the Negro bourgeoisie, were toward the upper class. That is why his earlier poems expressed faithfully the aspirations of the Negro worker, while both his later poems and his novels reflect his desire to be with the class which had adopted him. Dunbar's three novels, *The Uncalled, The Love of Landry,* and *The Fanatics,* deal in a most artificial manner with the trivialities of parasitic whites. In the first two there are no Negroes at all, and in the third book black workers are used only to create 'atmosphere.' " This leaves out of account of course the fourth novel, *The Sport of the Gods,* in which the chief characters are Negroes, but no one would contend that that would materially affect the point of the criticism.

These two opinions may be taken as representative of the best of adverse criticism in recent years and neither one can be wholly gainsaid. We have seen how in such a poem as "To the South" Dunbar missed an opportunity for forthright expression; and not one of his four novels was an unqualified success. He would doubtless have been startled, however, if he had been told that he was not sufficiently sympathetic with the Negro worker, and it was certainly not his intention to look simply to the past. "I greet the dawn and not a setting sun," he said; and he followed with eagerness every forward-looking movement of his people. One must consider also the total impress of his achievement. Like Byron he had something of the power of a bard to inflame a people. Less artistic than Keats, he was more dynamic. Above everything that he wrote was he himself, and when all discount is made, the fact remains that he inspired the young Negro of the country more than any other man who ever lived. Dr. W. S. Scarborough said of him, "In his song he has helped pave the way for a future for his race. He has hewn out a path, has trodden the ground for others to follow, and what was possible in his case is possible for others." That certainly seems to have been the impression that he made in his time.

It thus appears that Dunbar, like any other man, must be esteemed for what he was rather than judged by what he was not; and his merits are clear and unmistakable. It is easy enough to look at him after forty years and see some things that he might have done differently, even some that he might have done better; but to be severe with him because he did not voice our age would be the same as to blame Riley for not writing Sandburg's poems. In his own way he sang his song, and there were those who were happy to listen.

It has often been remarked that his chief qualities are humor and pathos, and as a poet of the people he has been compared with Burns. The comparison is apt, and yet it is easy to emphasize it unduly. There was in Dunbar something that, as Whitlock said, soared above race and touched the heart universal. He came on the scene at a time when America was just being launched on the machine age and when the country was beset by problems. Against the bullying forces of industrialism he resolutely set his face. In a world of discord he dared to sing his song, about nights bright with stars, about the secret of the wind and the sea, and the answer one finds beyond the years. In doing this, he vindicated the spirit of youth —youth that is the same in all climes and all ages, youth that believes in itself and is not overcome. Above the dross and the strife of the day, he asserted the right to live and love and be happy. That is why he was so greatly beloved, and why he will never grow old. This above all else is his title to fame.

APPENDIX

The Praise of Dunbar

DUNBAR's remarkable rise to prominence stimulated many other men, and there were numerous tributes, in verse as well as prose, especially at the time of his passing. Some of these were better in intention than in execution, but others were of very different quality. A few of the stronger poems are given herewith.

James D. Corrothers (1869-1917), a Negro writer who attracted some attention about the turn of the century, after a youth of hardship succeeded in getting an education and entered on the work of the ministry. He published *Selected Poems* (1907), *The Dream and the Song* (1914), and *In Spite of the Handicap* (1916), an autobiography. Professor Waldo H. Dunn, well known for his book *English Biography*, has for several years been in charge of the work in the department of English at the College of Wooster (Ohio). While still a young man, just completing his college course at Yale, he was acquainted with Dunbar. Lucian B. Watkins (1879–1921) was one of the many Negro poets whose hopes are not fully realized. He was from Virginia and published *Voices of Solitude* (1907). His health was shattered in the World War and he died in Fort McHenry Hospital. Walter Everette Hawkins (1886–) is a poet of strong racial feeling. Born in Warrenton, N. C., he later went to Washington, D. C., and worked in the postoffice; he now lives in Brooklyn. In 1909 he brought out in Washington *Chords and Discords,* reissued in 1920 in Boston. Charles Fred. White was one of the founders and the heavy bass singer of the Umbrian Glee Club, which once presented Dunbar in recital at Quinn Chapel, Chicago. His tribute to the poet was included in his book, *Plea of the Negro Soldier, and a Hundred Other Poems* (Boston, 1908). Scofield Thayer was editor of the *Dial* at the time his poem appeared. It was reprinted in the *Literary Digest* (January 23, 1926). Mme. Silvia Margolis is a talented author of Dayton, Ohio. Her chief interests are Poetry and Humanity, and she has devoted her life very largely to the abolition of prejudice. Miss Angelina W. Grimké was for some years a teacher in the Dunbar High School, Washington, D. C., and has published, aside from various poems, *Rachel,* a dramatic work in three acts (Boston, 1921).

Paul Laurence Dunbar

BY JAMES D. CORROTHERS

He came, a dark youth, singing in the dawn
Of a new freedom, glowing o'er his lyre,
Refining, as with great Apollo's fire,
His people's gift of song. And thereupon,
This Negro singer, come to Helicon,
Constrained the masters, listening, to admire,
And roused a race to wonder and aspire,
Gazing which way their honest voice was gone,
With ebon face uplit of glory's crest.
Men marveled at the singer, strong and sweet,
Who brought the cabin's mirth, the tuneful night,
But faced the morning, beautiful with light,
To die while shadows yet fell toward the west,
And leave his laurels at his people's feet.

Dunbar, no poet wears your laurels now;
None rises, singing, from your race like you.
Dark melodist, immortal, though the dew
Fell early on the bays upon your brow,
And tinged with pathos every halcyon vow
And brave endeavor. Silence o'er you threw
Flowers of love.   Or, if an envious few
Of your own people brought no garlands, how
Could Malice smite him whom the gods had crowned?
If, like the meadow-lark, your flight was low,
Your flooded lyrics half the hilltops drowned;
A wide world heard you, and it loved you so,
It stilled its heart to list the strains you sang,
And o'er your happy songs its plaudits rang.

To Paul Laurence Dunbar

BY WALDO H. DUNN

Dunbar, thy harp-strings now are silent all,
And only sadness and a gloom remain,
Which fill my heart with truest, deepest, pain,
To know thou'rt gone, forever past recall;
And yet 'tis best that from the harsh world's thrall
Thou'rt passed; Earth left, how much of Heav'n they gain,
Who knew life's sorrow and its hopes how vain;
God's glory now doth on thy vision fall!
Thou sangst the joys and pains, the hopes and fears
Of all thy race's hard and bitter past,
Of such a sweetness that thy songs will last,
And brighten all the path of future years;
I, of an alien race, am moved to tears,
And on thy grave do all my garlands cast.

Ballade to Paul Laurence Dunbar

BY LUCIAN B. WATKINS

We would not call you, Dunbar, from your rest,
   For you were weary when you softly sang
The lullaby that soothed your love-sweet breast,
   And o'er the raptured world divinely rang,
   Amid the storms of Life's tumultuous clang,
Of battle-thunders in the fateful night
   That hide the smiles of Heaven from our sight;—
   Lo, while you sleep the sleep of Paradise,
We seek the blessed morning and its light,
   "Ere sleep comes down to soothe the weary eyes."

ENVOI

Ah, Poet Paul! you sang and all is right.
We feel our souls expanding for the flight—
   Lord, help us breathe to Thee a prayer and rise
And touch Thy truth eternal on the height,
   "Ere sleep comes down to soothe the weary eyes."

Dunbar

BY WALTER EVERETTE HAWKINS

The Muses tuned his harp with song—
Too sweet a strain to linger long,
The tension of the chords too great
For longer life to compensate.
He lived and loved, a lamb at play,
He dreamed and sang his life away;
A genius of the lyric art,
He gave to man his all—his heart.
The world, unwilling to inspire,
Crushed his best music in his lyre,
And gave to broken rhyme the praise—
The merry music of his lays;
And yet he lifted up his race
And gave it undisputed place
Among the masters of the age,
And gave himself as heritage.

The chord is broken in the lyre,
Quenched is the Muse's vestal fire;
The oil that fed the vestal flame
Illumes in Heaven the Poet's name;
And still, sweet Singer, thou art near,
Thy merry music still doth cheer
The fireside, the camp, the road,
And gives a lightness to the load.
Sweet Spirit of a purer sphere,
We saw thee pass with holy tear;
But hope doth wring from tears their sting—
In better life thou still dost sing.

A Poem

BY SCOFIELD THAYER

Not Forgetting Paul Laurence Dunbar

Poets I have loved so deeply,
Poets I have loved so long,
Teach me, ah, gravely teach me
The wonder of broken song.

Teach me the language of moonlight
Which speaks on waters at Dawn,
That I may syllable moonlight
Ere my brief Dark is gone.

Teach me the error of Twilight,
The wilful change of the moon,
Teach me the malice of April,
Teach me the terror of June.

Teach me the error of Twilight,
Teach me to wander at Dawn,
Teach me the vagrant knowledge
Of why a heart was born.

Teach me to utter that pallor
Which is the lips of Day,
Teach me the small, grave words
Wherewith the flowers pray.

Teach me to fold my heart
In a little scrap of song,
Teach me to tie it gaily,
Teach me to weep long.

On the Death of Dunbar

BY CHARLES FRED. WHITE

Is Dunbar gone, forever and for aye?
  No, he is not! his soul has never died;
His spirit form is with us through our day;
  Nor in our night doth it desert our side.

Though sweet "Li'l' Gal" may weep, "Malindy" mourn,
  "The Party" veil its face with solemn crêpe
In sorrow for him of whom they were born;
  And though we, too, may weep at his sad fate;

Yet, one consoling thought remains to cheer
  Us in this hour of lamentation deep:
His soul yet lives, is with us year by year.
  He is not dead, for in our midst he sleeps

Enfolded 'tween the covers of his books.
  The old tree, torn with bullets, by the road
Still moans the story of its deadened looks;
  The "Ole Mule," with his lazy, human load,

Still plods along his weary, homeward way;
  "Malindy Sings" as sweetly to our mind;
The "Uncalled" hovers round us as to sway
  Our lives with "Lyrics," poetry and rhyme.

We need but to unfold his clothbound bier,
  To take him from his grave upon our shelves
And lend his inmost soul our closest ear,
  And Dunbar lives, and speaks, e'en as ourselves.

A life we mourn which late we oft extolled;
  A work unfinished, yet complete, we read.
Like his, our lives, our talents will unfold
  And bloom with beauty, if our hearts we heed.

Paul Laurence Dunbar—A Ballad

BY SILVIA MARGOLIS

I

"Paul," said his angel,
  "Little, black Paul,
Sing, no matter
  What befall!"

Hence, the child,
  Like an elf
Sang low, as if
  To please himself.

All things drab,
  And all things mean
His lowly songs
  Made white and clean.

His bitter bread
  And bitter meat
He dipped in song—
  And made them sweet.

And to his poor,
  Downtrodden race
He gave a sweetly
  Flowing grace.

Thus, the child
  Like an elf,
Sang low—as if
  To please himself.

Ere he tasted
  Acrid care,
Or guessed there was
  A Cross to bear.

II

But youth o'ertook
  Him on his way
And, unsealed
  His eyes one day:

Alone, upon
  A bank of dross
He screamed to wake
  And feel—his Cross.

His strength was mist,
  His song was moan:
The Cross was not
  His alone.

But all bowed down,
  And all bent low
Laid on him
  Their weight of woe.

And made his Cross
  A bitter thing
He felt the songs
  But could not sing.

III

Again the angel
  Whispered, "Paul,
Sing, no matter
  What befall!"

And tho his thirst
  Was deep and dire
And all about him
  Wells of mire—

Suddenly
  He overbrimmed
With visions he
  Had scarcely dreamed.

Like Springtime's touch
    On Winter's snow
Swells the current
    Of a river, so

Did now his spirit
    Overflow
In sudden streams
    Of light below.

Now, everywhere,
    The common sod
Flashed up to him
    The light of God.

Now, every mood
    In mead and mart
Made a poem
    In his heart.

He could not help
    But yield and sing—
He saw such beauty
    In each thing.

He saw such beauty
    Night and noon
He could but sing
    In perfect tune.

IV

But ah! the world—
    It is cold
To a Singer—
    As of old!

Colder still
    And deaf, alack!
To a Singer
    That is black!

Race-hatred pierced
  His tender breath,
And oft he cried
  For death! for death!

V

Once more the angel
  Whispered: "Paul,
Sing—no matter
  What befall!"

And the heart
  That lately bled
Once again
  His rhythm fed:

All the sorrow
  That he saw
Gave his songs
  A perfumed awe.

At every bit
  Of broken heart
Flowed the more
  His magic art.

VI

He made his songs
  Now, wide and deep—
There were so many
  Dreams to keep.

There were so many
  Hopes to hide . . .
He made his songs
  Now, deep and wide.

VII

And when he came
  To man's estate
The angel found
  No cause to rate:

Altho there was
  But a breath of him
He reached the heart
  Of life supreme:

Master now
  Of song and care
He learned to bleed
  And to forbear.

He learned to bleed
  And stand apart
In his warm
  Singing heart.

For, save a warm
  Singing heart—
He had no other
  Place or part.

He had no other
  Aim or art—
Save a warm
  Singing heart.

VIII

In the Heights
  Or on the Brink
He asked no other
  Food or Drink,

He asked no other
    Prize or Thing
But like a linnet—
    Lived to sing!

And like a linnet,
    All unknowing—
Whither may
    His songs—be flowing—

He gave them such
    Exceeding grace—
They found our Secret
    Hiding-place.

He wove them so
    Exceeding good—
They lit the flame
    Of Brotherhood!

To the Dunbar High School: A Sonnet

BY ANGELINA W. GRIMKÉ

And she shall be the friend of youth for aye:
Of quick'ning youth whose eyes have seen the gleam;
Of youth between whose tears and laughter stream
Bright bows of hope; of youth, audacious, gay,
Who dares to know himself a Cæsar, say,
A Shakespeare or a Galahad. The dream
To him is real; and things are as they seem,
For beauty veils from him the feet of clay.
How holy and how wonderful her trust—
Youth's friend, and yes, how blest. For down the west
Each day shall go the sun, and time in time
Shall die, the unborn shall again be dust;
But she with youth eternal on her breast,
Immortal, too, shall sit serene, sublime.

Aside from the poems there have of course been many tributes in prose. The following editorial paragraph from the *Boston Evening Transcript* of February 10, 1906, is representative of the more careful and appreciative comment at the time of the poet's death.

The death of Paul Laurence Dunbar is a loss to American letters. He was not, perhaps, a great poet, but he was a real one. His verse was genuine, serious and sweet. He wrote because he was moved to write. His poetry was an expression of his own spirit. And Paul Dunbar was a black man. His metrical grace and power could not be credited to any admixture of white blood. He was, perhaps, the most conspicuous exemplification that his race has given to this country of the Negro's possibilities along lines of spiritual expression and artistic development. Moreover, he wrote as the Negro feels and the Negro talks. He has given value and permanence to the folklore of the race in this country. He made no attempt to escape from his origin or environment. Both appealed to him; both commanded his sympathy, and from the life which he knew so well he drew his inspiration. He won recognition and public applause, not simply because his work was creditable to a black man, but because it would have been creditable to anyone. He gave form and beauty to the thoughts and expressions of a primitive but imaginative people, which even in their crudity are well worth preserving. Simple lives, quaint customs, the unsung loves, longings and aspirations of his race found in him a tuneful and prophetic voice. They became invested with new meaning and real dignity. They were given a soul. He was a voluminous writer. His vein was apparently an exhaustless one, and to the last it yielded bright products for the working. He was not as great a poet as Burns, but he was not less genuine and as true to his motive and his inspiration. He won a place in American literature of which he can not be deprived by prejudice, because its history would be incomplete without the new and fine element which he supplied.

Bibliography

THE prime materials for a study of the life of Dunbar are naturally those preserved in his home in Dayton, especially his scrapbooks; and much can be gained from conversation with those who knew him best. Some letters are available, one or two in manuscript in the Library of Congress, and others in a number of the *Crisis*. In a valuable work cited below, Mrs. Lida Keck Wiggins, of Springfield, Ohio, recorded the results of several visits; and the poet's wife, in a special article, gave her recollections of the influences in Nature that suggested different poems. Much also is revealed by intensive study of Dunbar's own writings, especially the poems and those of his articles giving his impressions of life and the world.

The following lists endeavor to enumerate all of the formal publications of Dunbar and the more important of the articles bearing on his life and work. They do not undertake the task of citing every article or poem as it first appeared in a newspaper or magazine. As the first two volumes of poems, privately printed, are now exceedingly rare, there is included a comparative study of the first three volumes.

I. PUBLICATIONS

(in the order of their appearance)

OAK AND IVY. Printed by the United Brethren Publishing House, Dayton, Ohio, 1893. (This is the date, but the book actually appeared a little before Christmas, 1892.)

MAJORS AND MINORS. Printed by Hadley & Hadley, Toledo, Ohio, 1895. (This is the date, but the book actually appeared early in 1896.)

LYRICS OF LOWLY LIFE, with an Introduction by W. D. Howells. Dodd, Mead & Co., New York, 1896.

THE UNCALLED, a Novel. Dodd, Mead & Co., New York, 1898. (Originally in *Lippincott's Magazine*, LXIV, 579-669, May, 1898.)

FOLKS FROM DIXIE, with illustrations by E. W. Kemble. Dodd, Mead & Co., New York, 1898.

LYRICS OF THE HEARTHSIDE. Dodd, Mead & Co., New York, 1899.

POEMS OF CABIN AND FIELD, illustrated with photographs by the Hampton Institute Camera Club and decorations by Alice Morse. Dodd, Mead & Co., New York, 1899.

THE STRENGTH OF GIDEON, and Other Stories, with illustrations by E. W. Kemble. Dodd, Mead & Co., New York, 1900.

THE LOVE OF LANDRY. Dodd, Mead & Co., New York, 1900.

THE FANATICS. Dodd, Mead & Co., New York, 1901.

CANDLE-LIGHTIN' TIME, illustrated with photographs by the Hampton Institute Camera Club and decorations by Margaret Armstrong. Dodd, Mead & Co., New York, 1901.

THE SPORT OF THE GODS. Dodd, Mead & Co., New York, 1902. (Originally in *Lippincott's Magazine*, LXVII, 515-594, May, 1901. Issued as THE JEST OF FATE, Jarrold & Sons, London, 1903.)

LYRICS OF LOVE AND LAUGHTER. Dodd, Mead & Co., New York, 1903.

IN OLD PLANTATION DAYS. Dodd, Mead & Co., New York, 1903.

WHEN MALINDY SINGS, illustrated with photographs by the Hampton Institute Camera Club; decorations by Margaret Armstrong. Dodd, Mead & Co., New York, 1903.

THE HEART OF HAPPY HOLLOW, illustrated by E. W. Kemble. Dodd, Mead & Co., New York, 1904.

LI'L' GAL, illustrated with photographs by Leigh Richmond Miner, of the Hampton Institute Camera Club; decorations by Margaret Armstrong. Dodd, Mead & Co., New York, 1904.

LYRICS OF SUNSHINE AND SHADOW. Dodd, Mead & Co., New York, 1905.

HOWDY, HONEY, HOWDY, illustrated with photographs by Leigh Richmond Miner; decorations by Will Jenkins. Dodd, Mead & Co., New York, 1905.

JOGGIN' ERLONG, illustrated with photographs by Leigh Richmond Miner and decorations by John Rae. Dodd, Mead & Co., New York, 1906.

THE LIFE AND WORKS OF PAUL LAURENCE DUNBAR, containing his complete poetical works, his best short stories, numerous anecdotes, and a complete biography of the famous poet by Lida Keck Wiggins, and an Introduction by William Dean Howells from "Lyrics of Lowly Life." J. L. Nichols & Co., Naperville, Ill., 1907 (?).

THE COMPLETE POEMS OF PAUL LAURENCE DUNBAR, with the Introduction to "Lyrics of Lowly Life" by W. D. Howells. Dodd, Mead & Co., New York, 1913.

SPEAKIN' O' CHRISTMAS and Other Christmas and Special Poems, with numerous illustrations. Dodd, Mead & Co., New York, 1914.

In addition to the more important works listed above, attention may be called to the following items:

England as Seen by a Black Man. *The Independent*, XLVIII (Sept. 16, 1897).

Manuscript letters to Edward F. Arnold in Library of Congress, Washington.

Unpublished Letters of Paul Laurence Dunbar to a Friend. *The Crisis*, XX (June, 1920), 73.

Negro Life in Washington. *Harper's Weekly*, XLIV (Jan. 13, 1900), 32.

Negro Society in Washington. *The Saturday Evening Post*, Dec. 14, 1901.

Uncle Eph's Christmas, a one act musical sketch, music by W. M. Cook. New York (?), 1900.

The Negro as an Individual. *The Chicago Tribune*, Oct. 12, 1902.

Representative American Negroes, pages 187-211 of The Negro Problem (a series of articles by Representative American Negroes of To-day). James Pott & Co., New York, 1903.

For ready reference the following grouping of the books, aside from *Complete Poems*, may be noted:

POEMS:
Oak and Ivy, 1893 (1892).
Majors and Minors, 1895 (1896).
Lyrics of Lowly Life, 1896.
Lyrics of the Hearthside, 1899.
Lyrics of Love and Laughter, 1903.
Lyrics of Sunshine and Shadow, 1905.

ILLUSTRATED VOLUMES OF POEMS:
Poems of Cabin and Field, 1899.
Candle-Lightin' Time, 1901.
When Malindy Sings, 1903.
Li'l' Gal, 1904.
Howdy, Honey, Howdy, 1905.
Joggin' Erlong, 1906.
Speakin' o' Christmas, 1914.

NOVELS:
The Uncalled, 1898.
The Love of Landry, 1900.
The Fanatics, 1901.
The Sport of the Gods, 1902.

STORIES AND SKETCHES:
Folks from Dixie, 1898.
The Strength of Gideon, 1900.
In Old Plantation Days, 1903.
The Heart of Happy Hollow, 1904.

II. COMPARATIVE STUDY OF
FIRST THREE VOLUMES

Oak and Ivy brought together 56 poems. Of these, 20 were used in *Lyrics of Lowly Life,* and 11 of the 20 were also in *Majors and Minors.* The following table may show at a glance the indebtedness of the second and third volumes to the first, the order being that of the appearance of the poems in *Oak and Ivy:*

	O & I	M & M	L L L
Ode to Ethiopia	x	x	x
A Drowsy Day	x	x	x
Keep a-Plugging Away	x		x
The Sparrow	x	x	x
October	x		x
Merry Autumn	x		x
Sunset	x	x	x
Hymn	x	x	x
A Banjo Song	x	x	x
The Ol' Tunes	x	x	x
The Old Apple-Tree	x		x
Whittier	x		x
After While	x		x
Melancholia	x		x
Life	x	x	x
Columbian Ode	x	x	x
The Meadow Lark	x	x	x
The Seedling	x	x	x
Nora: A Serenade	x		x
Night of Love	x		x

The following poems in *Oak and Ivy,* 17 in all and here given in alphabetical order, were rejected for both *Majors and Minors* and *Lyrics of Lowly Life* but included in the latter pages of *Complete Poems:*

A Career
An Old Memory
A Summer Pastoral
A Thanksgiving Poem
Christmas Carol
Evening
In Summer Time
James Whitcomb Riley
Love's Pictures

Nutting Song
On the Death of W. C.
On the River
Poor Withered Rose
The Old Homestead
To Pfrimmer
To the Miami
Worn Out

In *Lyrics of Lowly Life* are 105 poems. Of these, 20 first appeared in *Oak and Ivy*, and 74 were first in *Majors and Minors*. Thus only 11 first appeared in book form in *Lyrics of Lowly Life*. The matter may be stated differently. To the 74 that first appeared in *Majors and Minors* may be added the 11 that the table has shown were in all three volumes. There is thus a total of 85 brought over from *Majors and Minors* to *Lyrics of Lowly Life*. If to these are added the 9 that were brought over from *Oak and Ivy* but not used in *Majors and Minors*, we again have a total of 94 to be subtracted from 105. The following are the 74 that first appeared in *Majors and Minors*, the order being that of *Lyrics of Lowly Life:*

Ere Sleep Comes Down to
  Soothe the Weary Eyes
The Poet and His Song
Retort
Accountability
Frederick Douglass
The Lesson
The Rising of the Storm
A Prayer
Passion and Love
Promise and Fulfilment
Song

An Ante-Bellum Sermon
The Corn-Stalk Fiddle
The Master-Player
The Mystery
Not They who Soar
Ode for Memorial Day
Premonition
Retrospection
Unexpressed
The Rivals
The Lover and the Moon
Conscience and Remorse

Ione
Religion
Deacon Jones' Grievance
Alice
After the Quarrel
After a Visit
The Spellin'-Bee
A Border Ballad
An Easy-Goin' Feller
A Negro Love Song
The Dilettante
By the Stream
The Colored Soldiers
Nature and Art
When de Co'n Pone's Hot
Ballad
The Change has Come
Comparison
A Corn Song
Disappointed
Invitation to Love
He Had his Dream
Good Night
A Summer's Night
Ships that Pass in the Night
The Delinquent

Dawn
Dirge
Preparation
The Deserted Plantation
The Secret
The Wind and the Sea
Riding to Town
We Wear the Mask
One Life
Changing Time
Dead
A Confidence
Phyllis
Right's Security
If
The Song
Signs of the Times
Why Fades a Dream?
Speakin' o' Christmas
Lonesome
Growin' Gray
To the Memory of
    Mary Young
When Malindy Sings
The Party

III. CRITICISM

Books and Pamphlets

Brawley, Benjamin: The Negro in Literature and Art. Duffield
    & Green, New York, 1918, revised 1921, 1929, pp. 64-75
    in last edition. (See also article in *Dictionary of American
    Biography*.)

Dunbar, Mrs. Paul Laurence: Scarborough, W. S.; Ransom,
    Reverdy C.: Paul Laurence Dunbar, Poet Laureate of the
    Negro Race. Reprinted from the *A. M. E. Church Review*,
    Philadelphia, Penn. Not dated. (A pamphlet of 32 pages,

unique as including an account by the poet's wife of the influences in Nature that suggested various poems.)

Johnson, James Weldon (editor): The Book of American Negro Poetry. Harcourt, Brace & Co., New York, 1922, revised 1931, pp. 34-35, 49-52 in last edition.

Johnson, James W.: Along this Way. Viking Press, New York, 1933.

Kerlin, Robert T. (editor): Negro Poets and their Poems, pp. 37-41. Associated Publishers, Inc., Washington, D. C., 1923.

Locke, Alain (editor): The New Negro, An Interpretation. A. & C. Boni, New York, 1925, including "The Negro in American Literature," by William Stanley Braithwaite, originally in The Crisis.

Loggins, Vernon: The Negro Author: His Development in America, pp. 313-317, 320-324, 344, 352. Columbia University Press, New York, 1931.

Pearson, Paul M.: Paul Laurence Dunbar, a Tribute. (No date, but reprinting articles from Talent for March, 1906, and Feb., 1904, also several poems.)

White, Newman Ivey, and Jackson, Walter Clinton (editors): An Anthology of Verse by American Negroes, pp. 11-14. Trinity College Press, Durham, N. C., 1924.

NEWSPAPERS AND MAGAZINES

Alexander's Magazine (formerly published in Boston), May, 1906. Paul Laurence Dunbar, by Edward H. Lawson.

Athenaeum, The, Nov. 29, 1902. Review of The Jest of Fate, English edition of The Sport of the Gods.

Book-Buyer, The (new series), Vol. XXIII, p. 26, Aug. 1901. Review of Folks from Dixie, with comparison with Chesnutt.

Bookman, The.
> VIII, p. 338, Dec. 1898. Across the Colour Line, by Grace Isabel Colbron, largely review of The Uncalled.
>
> XII, p. 512, Jan. 1901. Review of The Love of Landry.
>
> XXIII, p. 122, April, 1906. Mr. Dunbar's Best Book (The Sport of the Gods); p. 185. Tribute by W. D. Howells.

Charities Review, VII, p. 828, Dec. 1897. Special article reviewing Lyrics of Lowly Life, by C. Breckenridge Wilmer.

Crisis, The.
> XVII, p. 72, Dec. 1918. Ballade to Paul Laurence Dunbar, by Lucian B. Watkins.

XXXIX, p. 118, April, 1931. "De Lawd" on Broadway, by Olyve L. Jeter (discussing early association of Dunbar and Richard B. Harrison).

Commercial Advertiser, The, New York, Feb. 13, 1899. Report of meeting at the Waldorf-Astoria for benefit of Hampton Institute.

Current Literature, XL, p. 400, April, 1906. Chief Singer of the Negro Race.

Harper's Weekly, XL, p. 630, June 27, 1896. Review of *Majors and Minors* by W. D. Howells in "Life and Letters." (This is the notable review that directed the attention of the country to Dunbar.)

Journal of Negro History, XVII, pp. 400-408, Oct. 1932. Some Personal Reminiscences of Paul Laurence Dunbar, by Edward F. Arnold.

Lippincott's Magazine, LXXVII, p. 512, April, 1906. The Passing of Dunbar (poem), by S. X. Floyd.

Reading (Pa.) *Times, The,* Jan. 20, 1933. Dunbar, Negro Poet, Lives Again. (Report of address and reading by Mrs. Alice Dunbar Nelson at Washington Street Presbyterian Church, Reading, Pa., January 19, 1933.)

Southern Workman, The.

XXVI, p. 4, April, 1897. Review of *Lyrics of Lowly Life.*

XXIX, p. 487, Aug. 1900. Review of *The Strength of Gideon.*

XXX, p. 557, Oct. 1901. Review of *The Sport of the Gods* as in *Lippincott's Magazine.*

XXXII, pp. 629, 630, Dec. 1903. Reviews of *In Old Plantation Days* and *When Malindy Sings.*

XXXIII, pp. 692, 693, Dec. 1904. Reviews of *Li'l' Gal* and *The Heart of Happy Hollow.*

XXXIV, p. 628, Nov. 1905. Review of *Howdy, Honey, Howdy.*

XXXV, p. 136, March, 1906. Editorial comment.

L, pp. 227, 469, May and Oct. 1921. The Plantation Negro in Dunbar's Poetry and Dunbar's Poetry in Literary English, by Charles Eaton Burch.

LIX, p. 189, April, 1930. Dunbar Thirty Years After, by Benjamin Brawley.

Springfield (Mass.) *Sunday Republican, The,* March 4, 1906.

Paul Laurence Dunbar's Work, by George W. Forbes (termed by the editors "a remarkable personal and literary estimate").

Star, The, Kansas City, Mo., Jan. 5, 1902. An interview, good for personalia, practically the same being in *The Evening Star,* Washington, D. C., Oct. 1, 1904, signed Gilberta S. Whittle.

Times, The, Washington, D. C., Sept. 25, 1898. Review of *Folks from Dixie.*

Times-Herald, The, Chicago, Oct. 14, 1900. Reproduction of sketch by Professor P. M. Pearson.

Voice of the Negro, The (formerly published in Atlanta).

    III, p. 50, Jan. 1906. Den of a Literary Lion, by Mrs. L. K. Wiggins.

        pp. 173, 184, March, 1906. Editorial comment and tribute of a sonnet by James D. Corrothers.

        pp. 244, 265, 271-278, April, 1906. Editorial comment, poem by Benjamin Brawley, and important article by Mary Church Terrell.

        pp. 408, 437, June, 1906. The Service of Dunbar, by George Davis Jenifer, and sonnet by Waldo H. Dunn.

Question has arisen as to the minister who performed the ceremony at the marriage of Paul Laurence Dunbar and Alice Ruth Moore on March 6, 1898. The poet in a letter to Dr. Tobey referred to "the bishop," and this has frequently been taken to refer to Bishop Henry C. Potter of the Protestant Episcopal Church. The author was otherwise informed by Mrs. Alice Dunbar Nelson, who read the manuscript of the present work some months before her death. The minister was Bishop W. B. Derrick of the A. M. E. Church, as is stated on page 63. Official verification has been given by a photostatic copy of the marriage certificate on file in the Bureau of Records of the Department of Health of the City of New York. The poet's birthplace was given as Dayton and his place of residence as Washington. His age was 25, his father's name Joshua Dunbar, and his mother's maiden name Matilda J. Burton. The bride's birthplace was New Orleans and her place of residence Brooklyn. Her age was 22, her father's name Henry Moore, and her mother's maiden name Patsy Wright. The witnesses were Joseph Derrick and J. H. Henderson.

Index